Contents

Introduction

Do you like Minecraft? Do you think it would be cool control electricity? **Have you ever wondered how a computer works?** Would you like to design and build worlds that move and interact however you'd like them to?

If you answered yes to any of these questions, you would undoubtedly enjoy the powerful world of Redstone.

Redstone is a special system of power and mechanisms that is part of the world's most popular video game, Minecraft. Essentially, Redstone simulates a (slightly) simplified version of real-life electricity, which players of Minecraft can use to power infinite creations of their own designs. These creations can do just about anything you could want in the game of Minecraft, from reducing previously tedious tasks like farming and hunting into things that happen at the push of a button, to creating devastating player-vs-player weapons, to even virtually simulating massively complex real-life electronic machines such as computers.

Introduction

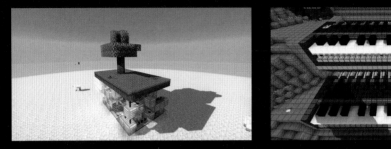

From concise and useful builds like the hidden tree door on the left to the monster, super-complex, fun builds like the piano on the right, Redstone is a fascinating material with near infinite uses.

Redstone is, to be blunt, the most powerful and creative tool ever created inside of a video game. Learning how to use Redstone is not only what separates a well-versed Minecraft player from a true expert, it's also just a step away from learning how electrical engineering works in reality. In fact, as a system that relies on rules grounded in the real-world concepts of logic and electrical systems, Redstone is a system that is both incredibly fun to learn, and which will seriously stretch the brain of anyone who takes the time to dive into it and learn its mighty secrets.

And that's where this book comes in. As a system whose basic rules are simple, but which is certainly one of the hardest things to learn in all of video games, Redstone engineering is quite intimidating when you first come across it. This book is here to show you that not only is learning Redstone possible for any video game player out there, it's also a heck of a lot of fun, and something which you can start learning in just a few minutes.

That being said, becoming a true master Redstone engineer who can craft up mind-boggling works of mechanical and logical genius is a task that takes time, dedication, and not just a little bit of trial-and-error. With this book, however, we're going to start you off on the path to Redstone mastery the right way, easing you into the subject and teaching you all of the tricks and lessons of the great Redstone creators so that, by the end, you'll be well on your way to creating such awesome constructs as slick automatic doors, devastating rapid-fire scattershot TNT and, yes, even simulations of actual computer systems inside of a video game.

It's an epic task, but one that's guaranteed to leave you smarter, not to mention turning you into the best Minecraft player of anyone you know.

If you're ready to start thinking in a new way and to begin to control the fabric of the virtual world of Minecraft, turn these pages and start getting familiar with Redstone- the most powerful and complex system that ever existed inside a video game.

The **Basics**

Ready to start your journey to becoming a master of all that is Redstone? Well then, let's dive right on in and get familiar with the basics of the Redstone world!

Before we do so, however, let's talk for a moment about how to best use this book to get the most out of it and to become the most knowledgable Redstone engineer you can:

How to Use This Book

Redstone is a massive topic, almost infinitely so because there are always players finding new ways to use it, and also because it often gets updated when Minecraft itself gets an update. This book is not meant to contain every single piece of information about Redstone, as that would be impossible, at the worst, or require a book that was a few thousand pages longer at best.

What this book is meant to do is to give you all of the basic information you need to begin learning how to use Redstone in the easiest and most pain-free way we can teach it to you. We want to make Redstone fun and inviting, and to dispel the air of intimidation and difficulty that often surrounds the subject.

We'll take you from the very most basic concepts of Redstone, starting here in this chapter, and as we go through the book, we'll add a little more with each chapter, stopping along the way to test out the ideas we present with some fun builds and cool applications.

We suggest that you approach this book from one end to the other, working through each chapter in turn and learning its lessons before moving on to the next. By the end of the book, we'll have you building some pretty highly advanced Redstone constructions and starting to think like a real Redstone engineer!

That being said, these concepts are also very complex, and there's a lot of information to internalize, so we'd also make one more suggestion for how to have the best and most successful Redstone learning experience:

Don't worry about getting it all perfect. Even the best Redstone engineers out there took a long time to understand and memorize this information, and there's no rush to do so. The best way to learn Redstone is to read through this book and test out the different builds, and then to just keep messing around with the stuff, referring back to the book when you need to know something. Over time, you'll start to naturally remember the nitty gritty details of Redstone items, rules and concepts without having to look them up, so there's no need to get discouraged if you keep having to look back at the book as you go.

In fact, we'd even suggest seeking out more resources on Redstone as well, such as watching videos online or finding other players to learn from. This book is meant to be your introduction to the world of Redstone and a handy reference guide, but we won't have our feelings hurt if you need to seek out a little extra help! The goal here is to help you learn Redstone, and we are simply trying give you as many resources in these pages as possible to help you do that.

One final note before we get going: Almost everything we talk about in this book assumes that you are playing in Creative Mode. This is because the builds take very, very many items of different types, and while you might have them in your Survival World, they will be pretty expensive. Additionally, Creative Mode allows you to fly and to turn off hostile mobs, allowing you to be able to learn in peace. We can't suggest doing this enough to learn Redstone's rules. Additionally, this book is primarily focused on the full version of Minecraft as it is on the PC and Mac. This is because the console versions do not contain all Redstone items quite yet, but they are being updated frequently. If you are playing on a console, you'll have to wait to try some of these concepts until the updates happen, but the basic rules and many of the builds are still the same and will work.

With that in mind, let's get into this!

The Concept

In a nutshell, Redstone is a system that uses power signals to cause something to happen in the game of Minecraft. This "something" could be as simple as opening a Door or turning on a light, or it could be something a bit more complex like causing a mechanism such as a Piston to activate and interact with the world, or it could be as complex as causing a mini-game to begin. A simple Redstone power signal can even cause something as intricate and massive as a player-built Redstone simulation of a computer to turn on and function!

Redstone power is somewhat like real-life electricity, and thinking of it like this is very useful, especially when first starting out with the stuff. Here are the ways in which Redstone and real-world electricity are similar:

- Redstone has an ON state and an OFF state.

- Redstone signals can have various levels of power, in the case of Redstone it goes from 0-15.

- Redstone signals can be carried through a Minecraft world through items called Redstone Dust (as well as others) that are very similar to real-life wires.

- A powered Redstone signal that is "wired" up so that it runs into certain items in the game called "mechanisms" will give those mechanisms power and cause them to activate.

- Redstone can be used to build "circuits" that function in much the same way as real-life circuits function in computers and other electronics.

There are, however, quite a few ways in which Redstone and normal electricity differ, and they are equally important:

The power that Redstone builds use is not always held in a storage unit like a battery, or piped through from the outside, but is instead almost always created by the items that toggle the power ON and OFF. To further explain the difference, a real-world light switch controls electric power, but it does not create the power. In Minecraft, Levers, which are very similar in look to light-switches, can control Redstone power, but they also create that power themselves. Redstone items that create power are called "power components," and there are many types of these, including two that do act somewhat like a battery and/or permanent power source (Redstone Torches and Blocks of Redstone).

Redstone power signals only go 15 blocks in one direction before their power signal fades away. To get it to go farther, it must be boosted. This is actually similar to real electricity, except that the rules that govern the distance of real electric signals are far more complex.

Redstone signals can and often are influenced by the passage of time. This is also actually similar to real electricity, but again there is a major difference. This time the difference is that the time delays on real electricity are often so fast that we do not even recognize them, while in Redstone this is essentially slowed way down so that players can manipulate and use these delays. Time in Redstone is measured in "ticks," where each a tick happens 10 times a second, or once every 0.1 seconds in real time. Redstone components and mechanisms update their status every tick, checking to see if their inputs have changed in any way, and when the input does change, they respond by activating, deactivating or performing a special action. Note: time in the rest of Minecraft also operates on "ticks," but a regular Minecraft ticks happen 20 times a second, making them twice as fast. This often confuses players who are aware of regular Minecraft ticks, so it's a good idea to note the difference here. Additionally, when we refer to "ticks" from here on out in this book, we are referring exclusively to Redstone ticks.

When you know how to use these and the many other rules of Redstone together, you will be able to build incredible contraptions and systems, and the range of things you can do in everyone's favorite builder game expands in a huge way. In fact, Redstone is considered by many players to be the pinnacle of Minecraft knowledge, and many of the things that people build in the game that will cause less-experienced players to scratch their head and wonder how it even happened are made with Redstone.

The Components

Redstone is possible because of certain items and blocks in the game and the way they work together. In the next chapter, we'll look at each and every one of these very closely and give you all the details of how they work and what they're used in, but for now let's break the various Redstone components down into their most simple forms and talk about how they relate.

All Redstone items fall into one of the following categories:

1. Power & control components (usually just referred to as power components)
2. Transmission components
3. Mechanisms
4. Basic blocks
5. Rails and Rail-related items
6. Other items that interact with Redstone

In its most simple form, a Redstone build will have a power component and a mechanism, but most Redstone builds use items from at least three of these categories, and some can even use many items from all of these categories.

Let's take a second to get the basics of how the first three of these components interact

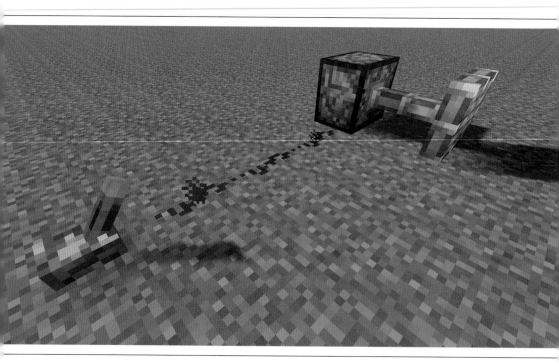

This is the basic Redstone setup: power component, wire and mechanism.

with each other set in our minds. A typical simple Redstone build starts with a power component, which sends a power signal out. This is often carried by transmission components to either other Redstone circuits or to mechanisms. When mechanisms receive an ON power signal, they activate.

Somewhere in this process of sending a power signal from power component>transmission component>mechanism, the signal may interact with basic blocks of the game. What we mean by this is blocks that are usually used for building purposes, such as Cobblestone, Dirt, Wool, Glass, etc. There are two important types of blocks when it comes to Redstone, and they interact with Redstone in different ways:

Opaque blocks: "Opaque" is a word that means an object through which light does not travel. In Minecraft, this definition usually applies as well. Opaque blocks are important to Redstone because they can be powered by a Redstone signal. When a block is "powered," this means that a Redstone signal is going into it, and that Redstone mechanisms, as well as Repeaters and Comparators (more on these in the Items chapter), will be activated by the block. This property of allowing Redstone signals to travel through themselves makes opaque blocks very important to Redstone.

Some transparent blocks (left) and some opaque blocks (right).

Transparent blocks: As you might guess "transparent" blocks are typically those that can be "seen through" in the game, though this term also refers to a few such as Glowstone and Slabs that the game merely treats as transparent, though they themselves block vision. In terms of Redstone, transparent blocks are important because they do not take a Redstone power signal, even if one is going straight into them. This makes transparent blocks very useful to separate and block currents in Redstone building.

Our final two types of Redstone items (Rail items, and other interactable blocks) are not nearly as core to Redstone concepts and building as the first four, though they can be integral parts of specific Redstone builds. These are essentially specialty items that can be used to create very specific results, as opposed to items that you'll be using in every build. More on these in the next chapter; all you really need to do now is to be aware that Rails and rail-related items as well as a few unique items can also interact with Redstone builds.

Putting it All Together for the First Time

Okay! So we know a bit about what Redstone is, we know a few of its rules, and we know the basic types of items that are used in Redstone builds, so it's time to actually test the stuff out!

We'll wrap this first chapter up by doing some small Redstone placement, and talk a bit about what's happening with each thing we do. Open up your Minecraft, get a new world started in Creative Mode, and let's play with a little Redstone.

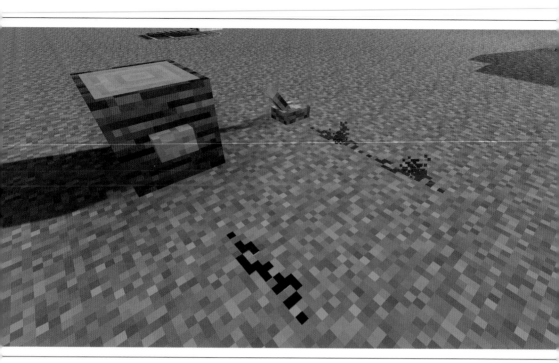

1. Component + Redstone Dust

First thing's first: let's see some Redstone actually powered up. Put a Lever, a Button (either kind) and some Redstone into your inventory. Place the Lever on the ground, and then place Redstone Dust on the ground right next to it. Now scoot over a bit and place the Button on a block (any opaque block is fine) and place Redstone Dust on the ground right in front of this. Make sure this second Dust is not touching the first and is not adjacent to the Lever.

Now, activate the Lever. See how the Redstone Dust lights up when you flick the Lever? This means it's powered, and that the power state is constant. If you want to turn it OFF, just flip the Lever to the other state. Now press the Button. See the difference? For the Button, the Redstone was only powered for a brief moment, and then it went off. This example is just to show you how Redstone Dust can be powered, and that different power components power it differently (in this case a constant signal vs. a temporary one).

2. Trying A Mechanism

Now flip your Lever OFF, and then put a Piston into your inventory. Place the Piston down adjacent to the Redstone Dust you placed next to your Lever, and then flip the Lever ON. As you can see, as soon as you flip the Lever, the Piston will activate, extending. This is the simplest form of a Redstone build (perhaps your first ever!). All that's happening here is that the Lever is providing a signal, the Dust is carrying the signal to the Piston, and the Piston is recognizing that it is powered and is firing. Though most Redstone builds get much more complicated than this, essentially this is what is happening at the basic level in almost all Redstone creations.

3. Powering An Opaque Block

Next, get a second Piston in your inventory, as well as a Redstone Torch and an opaque block. Move away from the Redstone items you have already placed, and put the opaque block down on the ground. Place a dot of Redstone Dust on the ground adjacent to the block (not on top of it though, for now), and then place the Redstone Torch on the opposite side of this Dust from the block. Now, go around to the opposite side of the block, and place the Piston down adjacent to this side of the block so that it is touching the block. For this example, make sure that the Piston is not adjacent to the Dust. You'll notice that the Piston also fires in this situation. This is because the block it is on is now "powered," which we talked about earlier in this chapter. The Redstone Torch, in this case, is providing the power signal to the Dust, which goes into the block and powers it, which then transfers the power to the mechanism. In this way we can see how powering blocks works and can be useful in Redstone.

4. Making Things More Complex With A Repeater

We're going to look at a very basic example of how we can make a Redstone build more complex for our final example. We'll need another Piston, another Lever and a Redstone Repeater for this one. Move away from your other Redstone builds, and place your Lever down on the ground. Put one dot of Redstone Dust adjacent to this Lever, and then stand on that Dust so that you are facing the opposite direction of the Lever. Aim down at the block on the opposite side of the Dust from the Lever while still standing on the Dust, and place your Repeater down. Now place the Piston on the block just after the Repeater, so you have a line of items that goes Lever>Dust>Repeater>Piston. Now flip the Lever. As you'll see, the Redstone current will go through the Dust, hit the Repeater, and then a slight amount of time later the Piston will fire. One of the features of Repeaters is that they output a signal at a slight delay, which in this case causes the Piston to fire, but which also has many other uses. We'll get to those later, but for now just notice how we can make the standard Redstone configuration more complex with other items.

Alrighty, we've done a little Redstone! That wasn't so bad, was it? Now you've got a bit of experience with the stuff, are starting to understand how it works, and hey! You can even tell your friends that you've started using Redstone. Good job miner!

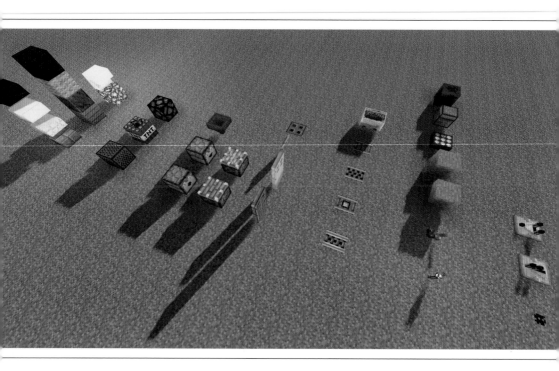

The **Items**

Knowing the items that are used in Redstone builds and how they interact with Redstone, and knowing this well, is the key to understanding Redstone. This chapter might not be the flashiest, most fun part of our little book, but it is perhaps the most important, as the information here is what will inform everything else you read. The better you know these items and their features, the better your Redstone builds will be, and the less time and energy you'll have to spend on each. Know these items, learn these items, love these items, profit.

Before we get to the things themselves, we should break down the different types of Redstone items and get an idea of what each type does, and why that's important:

The 6 Types of Redstone Items

Power & Control Components: (The Heart) These are the most important of the Redstone items, as they're what provide the Redstone power signal that everything else uses in a Redstone build. These come in a variety of types, with the difference between each being how they're activated, how much power they put out, what they power and how long they power it for.

Wires and Transmission Components: The second most important type of Redstone items, these are those items that move the power signal from a source of power to other parts of a Redstone build, whether it's a mechanism or another component. The simplest form of this is Redstone Dust, which simply moves the signal along a maximum of 15 blocks on its own, but the other items in the Repeater and the Comparator are essential to more complex builds.

Mechanisms: Essentially the items that "do something," whether that something is as simple as a Door opening or more complex like a Hopper sucking in and distributing items. These nearly all need power and activating them is often the "goal" of the Redstone build, but they can also simply be a small part of a Redstone build that causes something else to happen (such as how Pistons can be used to complete circuits).

Rails that Interact with Redstone: The Rails system in Minecraft also includes some items that interact with Redstone. This is primarily those Rail items that put out or interact with a power signal (Activator, Detector and Powered Rails), but Minecarts themselves are also part of the Redstone tool-box, as they can activate Activator Rails, among other things (like interacting with Hoppers).

Other Items that Interact with Redstone: This is a catch-all for items that don't create or transmit power as their primary function and aren't mechanisms, but which can be interacted with by a Redstone signal, or used in a Redstone build. These are less important in most builds compared to the items in the other sections, but they can be integral parts of some builds. For instance, the TNT can be an important part of certain builds like cannons.

Basic Blocks and Redstone: Some plain blocks interact with Redstone in particular ways. Most importantly, the way that "transparent" blocks (as opposed to the regular "opaque" block that is powered by a Redstone signal) interact with Redstone signals is very important.

These six categories pretty much cover the world of Redstone, so let's stop chatting about 'em and start getting familiar with the Redstone item pool.

KEY

✪✪✪✪ = The three core Redstone items
✪✪✪ = Very important and/or common Redstone items
✪✪ = Secondary, but still fairly commonly used Redstone items
✪ = Rare, or very simple Redstone items with a specific use

Note: We are leaving out Command Blocks, as the results they have on a map and a build are more about coding and understanding Minecraft's command language than it is about building with Redstone. If you're looking to learn more about that very complex topic, there are some great, if pretty dense, guides online.

Power & Control Components

These are what provide power to the rest of your build. Think of these like batteries that contain infinite power that you need to connect to your creations using wire (transmission components), and each of them sends out a signal (similar to powering with electricity) in different ways.

Redstone Torch ✪✪✪✪

Primary Feature: Gives a full Redstone power signal, which is a level 15 (out of 15) signal, which turns off if the block the Redstone Torch is on is or becomes a powered block

Powers:
- Block above Torch
- Dust adjacent
- Repeaters and Comparators adjacent and facing away from the Lever
- Mechanisms adjacent, above or below

Description: Ah the Redstone Torch, one of the three most common items in Redstone creation (the other two being Redstone and Redstone Repeaters). These guys are used in just about every Redstone build, and for good reason: Redstone Torches fully power Redstone Dust and mechanisms.

This is not the only way in which these glowy little dudes are useful, however. Redstone Torches also have two very special functions when it comes to opaque blocks, and these functions make Torches essential to most builds:

1. Redstone Torches do not power the block they are attached to. This is useful in many ways, for instance when you have a Redstone Torch on one side of a 1 block-thick wall, and there's a Redstone mechanism on the other side of the wall that you don't want the Redstone Torch to power.

2. Redstone Torches will be turned off if the block they are on is powered by something else. In other words, Redstone Torches that are on the top or side of a powered block (more on powered blocks in The Basics chapter) will have their signals inverted, meaning they no longer give out power to anything they were previously powering. This is incredibly useful in the creation of a huge variety of Redstone components, such as logic gates, as it can be

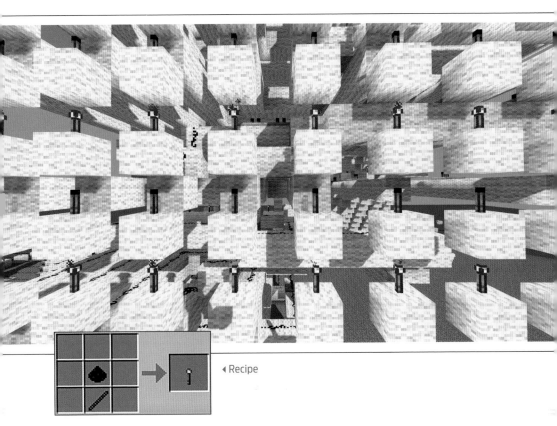

◄ Recipe

used to customize the way in which a specific line of power interacts with a Redstone build. For example, a common Redstone component called an AND Gate uses this inversion rule when attached to a Door in order to keep anyone from opening that Door without flipping two separate Levers. This makes the Door safer and more complex, and the AND Gate's ability to do this fully relies on the Redstone Torch inversion rule. More on gates like this in the Redstone Gates chapter.

Common Uses: Just about everything! One Redstone Torch on its own can power a mechanism or a line of Redstone Dust, or literally thousands could be used in complex builds such as Redstone computers. They can also be used to create a Torch ladder, which is one way of propagating a Redstone signal vertically in a compact space, something tricky to do.

Other Recipes Used In: Activator Rail, Redstone Comparator, Redstone Repeater

Block of Redstone ✪✪✪

Primary Feature: Provides full power signal, but it will not power opaque blocks of any kind.

Powers:
- Dust adjacent
- Repeaters and Comparators adjacent and facing away from the Redstone Block
- Mechanisms adjacent, above or below

Description: Blocks of Redstone are pure, unadulterated Redstone power. They power whatever is around them, except opaque blocks, which are unaffected by Blocks of Redstone. Blocks of Redstone can't be turned off, but they can be moved by Pistons and Sticky Pistons. In fact, attaching a Block of Redstone to a Sticky Piston can be an excellent way to inject or take away a power source from a specific section of your Redstone build when needed.

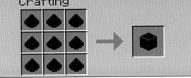

◄ Recipe

Redstone Blocks can be very useful when you want a guaranteed power source, but they are also fairly expensive (9 Redstone each), so they are more often used in Creative Mode as opposed to Survival. They can also be used as a way to store more Redstone in a Chest, as you can fit 576 Redstone in one full stack of 64 Blocks of Redstone.

Common Uses: Typically used in order to make builds more compact or where a Redstone Torch wouldn't work. For instance, Water can't move through a Block of Redstone, but it would destroy a Redstone Torch. A Redstone Torch would also power an opaque block above it, while a Block of Redstone would not, which you might want in some cases when layering Redstone builds on top of each other. Blocks of Redstone are also a lot easier to see than most other power sources, another useful feature in the right situation.

Other Recipes Used In: Can be converted back into 9 Redstone

Lever ✪✪✪

Primary Feature: When on, provides full power, but can also be turned off, cutting off the power.

Powers:
- Block it's on (if opaque)
- Dust adjacent
- Repeaters and Comparators adjacent and facing away from the Lever
- Mechanisms adjacent, above or below

Description: Levers not only provide power, they are also the first of our direct control components. This means that unlike Redstone Torches or Blocks of Redstone, the power output of a Lever can be directly controlled by changing the state of the Lever (meaning you can turn it on or off). While you can create this kind of alternating power output from a Torch

Crafting

◄ Recipe

or a Block of Redstone by building a special component to create this situation, Levers and other control components make the process of turning a Redstone power signal on or off much more efficient and easy to use.

Common Uses: Wherever an on/off switch for the power of a section of a Redstone build is needed. For instance, Levers can be placed on an opaque block adjacent to a Door. When the Lever is flipped on, the block the Lever is on will power the Door, causing it to open. When the Lever is switched off, the power to the block the Lever is on is turned off, and the Door closes, as it is no longer powered.

Button ✪✪✪

Primary Feature: Provides full power for just 10 ticks (1 second)

Powers:
- Block it's on (if opaque)
- Dust adjacent
- Repeaters and Comparators adjacent and facing away from the Button (the block the Button sticks out into)
- Mechanisms adjacent, above or below

The Items

Crafting

Crafting

◄ Recipe

Description: Another direct control power component, the Button acts just like the Lever, except that it only provides power for a period of 10 game ticks, or 1 real second. This is very useful for things that you only want in a powered state for a very short amount of time, like a Door, which will open when the Button is pressed but will close when the 10 ticks of power are over. One useful feature of Wooden Buttons in particular is that they can be activated by Arrows, whether shot by a player, a Skeleton or a Dispenser.

Common Uses: Where a short, simple burst of power is needed, such as having a Dispenser throw a single item, or a Piston extend for just 1 second.

Pressure Plate ✪✪

Primary Feature: Gives full temporary power similar to a Button. However, the power signal from the Pressure Plate activates due to something being on top of it (technically it is that the object collides with the Plate, but essentially it is because something or someone is on top of the Plate), and the power continues to come from the Plate as long as something is on the Plate. It powers for a minimum of 10 ticks (1 second).

Powers:
- Block it's on (if opaque)
- Dust adjacent
- Repeaters and Comparators adjacent and facing away from the Pressure Plate
- Mechanisms adjacent or above Pressure Plate (above only works with Wooden Pressure Plates and entities, as well as mobs, that are shorter than 1 block tall)

The Items

Recipes

Description: Pressure Plates are just like a Button, except they can only be put on the top of a block, and they can be activated much longer and only need pressure to activate, as opposed to being clicked on (or shot with an Arrow, in the case of the Wooden Button). This happens differently for various types of Pressure Plates, of which there are the following and the following methods of activation:

Wooden Pressure Plate: Activated by all entities (players and mobs, items of all kinds, Fishing Bobs, Arrows and even experience orbs)

Stone Pressure Plate: Activated only by mobs and players

Light Weighted Pressure Plate: Activated by at least 1 mob or player, but will put out a stronger signal with each additional entity of any kind on the Plate (1 entity = 1 power strength, 2 entities = 2 power strength, 3 = 3 etc.)

Heavy Weighted Pressure Plate: Activated by at least 1 mob or player, but will put out a much stronger signal with each additional entity of any kind on the Plate (1 entity = 1-10 signal strength, 2 entities = 11-20 signal strength, 3 entities = 21-30 signal strength etc.)

Common Uses: One use is for when you want a Redstone component to activate when either you or a mob runs over it, such as Doors opening when you run over a Pressure Plate, or a signal in your house activating telling you a mob is standing on a Pressure Plate outside your home. Another use is in complex builds where it would be useful for something to activate when enough items land on a Pressure Plate, such as causing a Piston to pull back and let Water temporarily flow over the ground in a mob grinder when enough mobs have been killed, washing all of the items they have dropped out of the grinder and to an area where you'd be able to pick them up.

Other Recipes Used In: Detector Rails

Tripwire Hook ✪✪

Primary Feature: When a complete Tripwire circuit is built, most entities (excepting some shot Arrows, and thrown Ender Pearls, Eyes of Ender and Potions) that move through the Tripwire will send out a full power signal. This lasts as long as an entity is colliding with the Tripwire, or for a minimum of 5 ticks, or 0.5 seconds.

Powers:
- Block both Tripwire Hooks are on (if opaque)
- Dust adjacent
- Repeaters and Comparators adjacent and facing away from the Detector Rail
- Mechanisms adjacent, above or below

Description: Sometimes pushing a Button or even running over a Pressure Plate won't be the ideal way to activate a Redstone build. In these cases, a nice Tripwire circuit may be the thing you need. This is basically a line that goes across the air or ground, and if anything besides the entities listed above collides with that line, it will power the Tripwire Hooks at

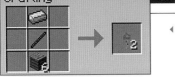

◀ Recipe

the ends of the Tripwire circuit. A working Tripwire circuit involves a Tripwire Hook placed on the side of one block, another placed on the side of another block in a direct line from the original Tripwire Hook, and then clicking on one of the Hooks while holding a piece of String. If the Tripwire Hooks are in the right place, and nothing is blocking the way (such as other blocks), you will see the piece of String go across the space between the Tripwire Hooks, and when you run through the String you'll hear the click of the Hooks being powered.

Common Uses: For places where it would be best for a Redstone mechanism or construct to activate anytime any entity crosses a certain line. An example would be a Dispenser launching a Potion at the user when they run past a certain part of their base, or for Dispensers to fire Arrows at a large area when anything crosses a long Tripwire in that area.

Daylight Sensor ★★

Primary Feature: Gives a power signal whose strength varies according to how much natural light the Daylight Sensor is exposed to. This is true up to the full light level of 15, at which point the Daylight Sensor is capable of reaching up to power level 8, and it then goes higher than 8 depending on the amount of time it has been exposed. It will then steadily become unpowered as it gets darker.

Powers:
- Block it's on (if opaque)
- Dust adjacent
- Repeaters and Comparators adjacent and facing away from the Daylight Sensor
- Mechanisms adjacent, above or below

Description: Daylight Sensors are the one power item that sends out power not based on a physical interaction (Levers, Buttons, etc.) or a constant state of having power (Redstone Torches and Blocks of Redstone), but instead on a non-physical entity, specifically the level of the light that is touching the Daylight Sensor. When powering Dust or Comparators, the amount of power going out from the Daylight Sensor and through the Dust or Comparator

Crafting

◄ Recipe

will be between 0-15 based on both the level of light and the amount of time exposed to light (see http://bit.ly/DaylightSensor for the full chart). Mechanisms attached to a Daylight Sensor will fire when light hits the Sensor at all, and attached Repeaters will instantly send a 15 power level signal. Note: it being night does not mean that the Daylight Sensor will immediately turn off, as there is still some light for part of the night. Daylight Sensors can also be turned to night time detectors by surrounding them in blocks or keeping them far from the sky, or they can be made into inverted daylight detectors by right-clicking the Sensor. This will make the Sensor act the opposite as it normally would, giving a full signal at night, a weak one during the day and none at noon.

Common Uses: Welp, just about anything you can think of that would depend on it being night or day to have power! Many Redstone builders use these to build automatic lighting systems for their homes and the areas around them at night, or to trigger a something such as a Redstone Torch that will give a visual notice that it's day even when deep down in a mine or another place where you wouldn't be able to see that it was such.

Trapped Chest ⭐

Primary Feature: Gives out a powered Redstone signal when opened.

Powers:
- Block(s) it's on (if opaque), power signal equal to the amount of players accessing chest (max of 15)
- Dust and Repeaters adjacent (and below for Dust only), power signal equal to the amount of players accessing chest (max of 15)
- Mechanisms adjacent, above and below

Note: Comparators treat the Trapped Chest as a typical Chest, reading the amount of items in it, and are not powered by it as a Redstone signal normally would power a Comparator.

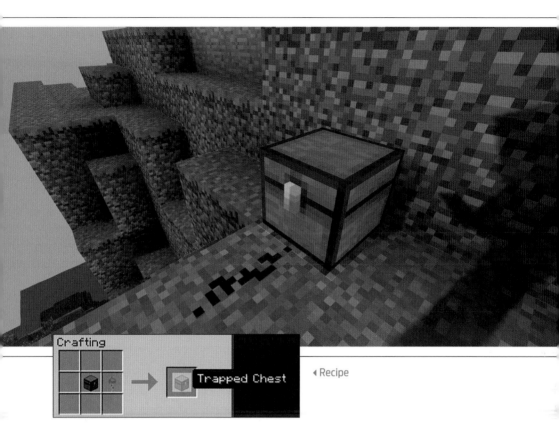

◄ Recipe

Description: The Trapped Chest is a unique power source in that it is almost exclusively used to give off an indication to a player that a Chest has been accessed. It will not only give out a power signal when the Trapped Chest is opened, but will also put out a signal of variable power based on how many people are looking into the Trapped Chest. This can even be hooked up to a memory circuit (more on this in the Advanced Wiring chapter) in order to know if anyone has accessed the Trapped Chest even when they no longer are doing so.

Common Uses: Mostly to keep tabs on your Chest and items and/or to make a trap for players that open the Trapped Chest (whether with TNT hooked up to it or otherwise), but could conceivably be hooked up to a more complex system if desired.

Wires and Transmission Components

These are the components that take a Redstone signal and actually put it out to things that can use it. This is what hooks everything up together and makes it possible.

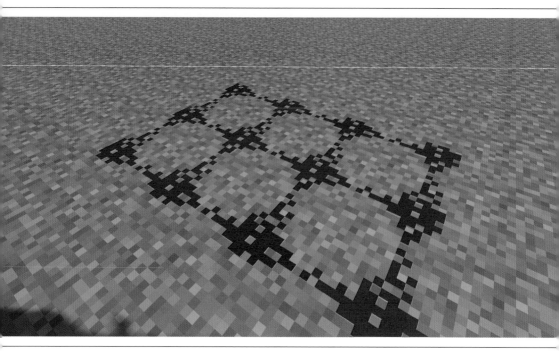

Redstone (aka Redstone Dust) ✪✪✪✪

Primary Feature: Transmits power in one direction, which can be routed to Redstone systems or used to activate Redstone mechanisms. When put down on a block, Redstone is called Redstone Dust. It's the soul of Redstone building, and it's what makes up the "wires" that connect everything Redstone together. Redstone is what makes it all work.

Powers:
- Block it's on (if opaque)
- Block in front of it (if opaque and in the direction the power is traveling)
- Dust adjacent
- Repeaters and Comparators adjacent and facing away from the powered Dust
- Mechanisms that the Dust directly "runs into" (will not power just by being adjacent to mechanisms)

The Items

Description: The main item of the Redstone world is, unsurprisingly, Redstone. To understand Redstone, imagine it as a real-life wire, which conveys power. In Minecraft, power sources like those in the previous pages (Levers, Buttons, Redstone Torches etc.) put out power like a battery, and Redstone Dust transmits it like a wire to other places.

You can lay Redstone down on all opaque blocks, upside down slabs, stairs and hoppers, and Glowstone, and it will show up as a dot on the top of the block if there is no other Redstone around it. It will also automatically "attach" to any Redstone that is immediately adjacent to it, as well as to Redstone on the blocks that are one block above or below and to the side (if there are any and there's nothing blocking the way).

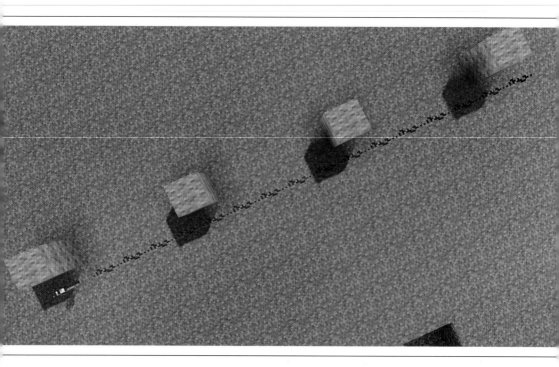

When power goes through Redstone Dust, it loses its power level by 1 for every block it travels through. The farthest a power signal can travel through one line of Redstone Dust from the source of power before it fades entirely to a 0 power level is 15 blocks. However, you can extend power to greater distances by adding Redstone Repeaters to a line of Redstone Dust, as well as by other methods.

Redstone will power mechanisms if power is going through it, but it has to be set up the right way. While Redstone automatically attaches to itself when adjacent to more Redstone Dust, it does not automatically face mechanisms correctly and must be built so that it directly powers the mechanism by facing into it. Powered Redstone Dust will also give weak power to any block it is either on top of or pointing directly at and adjacent to, but will never give full power this way.

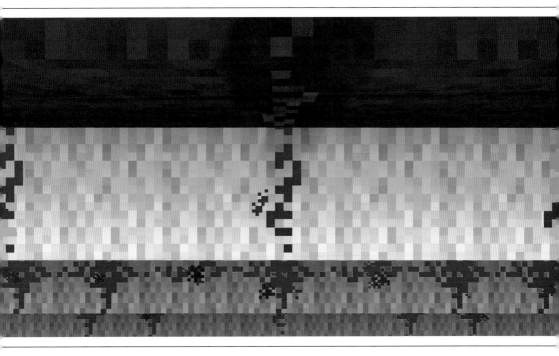

If all that weren't enough to make Redstone without a doubt the most complex item in Minecraft, the stuff is also used in many recipes, particularly for items with a function like Clocks (the item, not the Redstone build), Compasses and Redstone-specific items like Dispensers and Repeaters.

Common Uses: It's the most common Redstone item and the thing that is necessary for just about everything related to Redstone, so it's common to use it in all Redstone builds.

Other Recipes Used In: Block of Redstone, Clock, Compass, Detector Rail, Dispenser, Dropper, Note Block, Piston, Potions (Mundane Potion, Increased Duration, reverting other potions back to Level I), Powered Rail, Redstone Lamp, Redstone Repeater, Redstone Torch

Redstone Repeater ✪✪✪✪

Primary Feature: Boosts any incoming Redstone power signal to level 15 and sends it out in one direction while also slightly delaying the signal. The delay can be set from 1 to 4 ticks by right-clicking.

Powers:
- Block in front of it (if opaque and located in the direction that the power is moving)
- Dust, Repeaters and Comparators adjacent and facing in the same direction as the Repeater
- Mechanisms adjacent, above or below

Description: Another of the three big Redstone items (along with Redstone Torches and Redstone itself in Dust form), the Repeater is a triple function Redstone item. First, it transmits a signal just like Redstone Dust, except that on top of powering Dust, other Repeaters or Comparators, and mechanisms, it will also strongly power an opaque block in front of it (as opposed to Dust weakly powering such blocks). Second, it boosts whatever signal comes into it (from the back only) to a power level of 15. And third, it will always delay a signal for at least

◄ Recipe

1 tick, but can be set up to 4 ticks of delay by right clicking the Repeater (you can visually see it change its setting as the little torches on the Repeater move each time you click).

While the transmission and boosting properties make Repeaters automatically quite useful for bigger builds where a signal must be transmitted for long distances, the Repeater's delay feature adds to that usefulness in a huge way. That ability to keep a signal from reaching a certain part of a Redstone build for any amount of time you'd like (by directing the flow of power through multiple Repeaters) is used to create everything from simple functional Redstone builds like hidden doors, to basic Redstone clocks, to the most advanced Redstone computers.

Common Uses: Any build where you need to extend a Redstone signal or create just about any kind of complex circuit is going to need quite a few Repeaters, as will any build that needs any part of itself to be activated behind the exact moment you activate the power to the build. So basically all Redstone builds that are beyond the most simple.

Redstone Comparator ✪✪✪

Primary Feature: Multiple, but essentially it takes power signals in from behind and/or the left side and/or the right side and outputs the power signal based on the power levels of the various signals coming into the Comparator as well as based on which of its two settings it is on. It's either used to compare the power level of the incoming signals, subtract power from the level of the signal to its rear or, as a third feature, to put out a signal of a variable power level based on the amount of items inside of certain containers (such as Chests or Dispensers).

Description: Aaaaand now we come to by far the most complex single Redstone item: the Comparator (cool name right?). As the name suggests, the Comparator's main function is to "compare" various types of inputs and put out a specific power signal (or kill a power signal entirely) based on the input. Input can be from the sides and/or the back, or it could be from a container, from which the Comparator will read the amount of items and will put out a signal with a power level based on this number.

Let's break this complex item down first by the four possible ways that a Comparator can be "set":

Maintain state: This is when the Comparator only has a powered signal coming in from behind it, and in this setting it will simply output the same signal that is being input to it from behind. This does not mean, however, that there is nothing else hooked up to the Comparator: you could very well have a Comparator with inputs on the side as well that are simply turned off for the moment, which is very useful in certain builds.

Lowered, or Compare Signal state: In this state the Comparator has its front "torch" (on the Comparator itself) lowered and not lit up. This is for the "compare signal" setting of the Comparator. In this setting the Comparator looks at all signals that are coming into it (whether from the back, the left side, the right side or some combination of the three), and it will output a signal from the front that is the same as whichever incoming signal has the greatest power. So, if a signal with 12 power comes in from the left, and a signal with 4 power from the right, and a signal with 11 power from behind, the Comparator will output a signal with 12 power, because this is the strongest signal. This is another useful feature for very complex builds where you would like various parts of the Redstone build to put out a specific signal, and you would then like those signals interpreted by the Comparator, which then outputs a signal causing different things to happen depending on which signal at what level was chosen by the Comparator. This is a very powerful but difficult-to-master function that is typically reserved for very complicated builds.

Raised, or Subtract Signal state: When the Comparator is set so that the little torch on the front is raised and lit up, it's in "subtraction" mode. This setting also compares the signals coming into the Comparator, similar to the compare signal state, but instead of choosing the strongest signal to output, it will subtract the strength of the highest side signal from that of the rear signal. The minimum signal is 0 power, but it can be anything in between 0 and 15 (it will only be the max if the rear signal is 0 and one of the side signals is 15). So, with a left input signal of 4 and a right input signal of 6, a rear signal of 14 would have the 6 subtracted from it, and the Comparator would output 8.

Measure state: Comparators that are placed facing out from a container, or are facing out from a single block that is adjacent to a container, will be in "measure block" mode. This mode has the Comparator count how many items are in the container (works with any container, as well as with Cauldrons, End Portal Frames, Jukeboxes and Item Frames), and it will then put out a signal whose strength depends on the amount of items in the container. Empty containers put out a 0 signal, full containers a full 15 power signal, and the signal for any amount of items between full and empty is relative to the amount of total items a container could hold. The formula for signal strength is thus, with "truncate" meaning to cut off any fraction in the final number:

signal strength = truncate(1 + ((sum of all slots' fullnesses) / number of slots in container) * 14)

fullness of a slot = (number of items in slot) / (max stack size for this type of item)

It's a little complex, but it can be very useful for creating signals of various types and for building Redstone constructs that will tell you the fullness of a container at a glance.

The Items

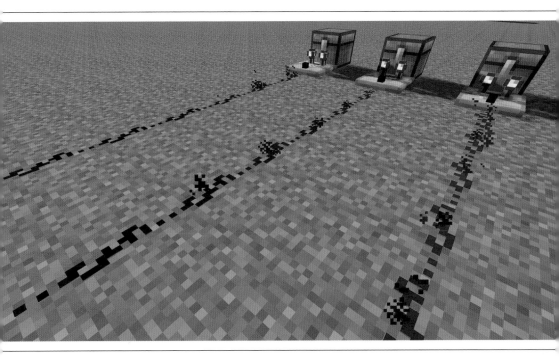

Items that aren't typical containers have different rules for the power output:
- Cauldrons put out a 0-3 signal depending on how much Water they contain
- End Portal Frames put out a 0 if empty and a 15 if containing an Eye of Ender
- Jukebox put out a different signal depending on what Record they are playing
- Item Frames put out a 0 signal if empty or 1-8 if containing an item and depending on the item's rotation

Common Uses: Complex ones, but basically when you want certain things to happen based on certain situations in your build. Whether that's based on the amount of items in Chests or whether you hook up a whole bunch of variable signals from different components to Comparators and want various outputs based on which components are activated, Comparators are the realm of the big, fancy, master engineer builds.

Mechanisms

The things that "do something" with your Redstone signal, though they can also be a part of the Redstone build that causes something else to be "done," such as helping to create complete circuits or activating power components.

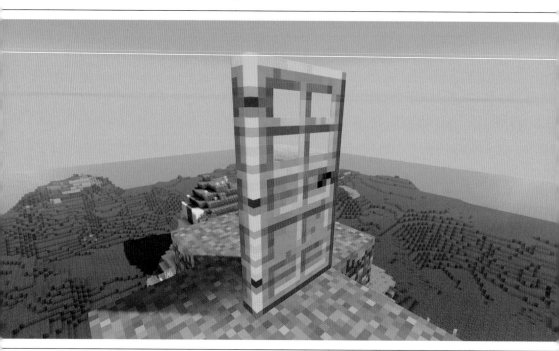

Door ✪✪

Primary Feature: Provides a 2 block tall, 1 block deep, 1 block wide barrier that is openable and closable, which allows players and even mobs to move from one area to the next when the Door is open, and not when it's closed. So basically, it's a plain ole door, but it can be activated (opened) by a Redstone power signal and closed when the signal is lost.

Powered by:
- Components adjacent, above or below
- Powered block adjacent, above or below
- Dust, Comparator or Repeater powered and facing in to the Door

Description: Doors are pretty darn straightforward when it comes to Redstone: basically a Redstone signal goin' in will open a Door, and no signal will close it. Iron Doors in particular actually require a Redstone signal to open at all and must otherwise be bashed down. Doors are mostly used simply as what they are (that being doors), as opposed to being a more complex part of a Redstone build.

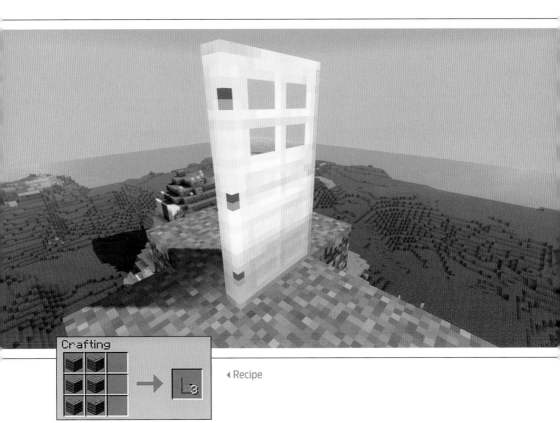

◀ Recipe

They also have a few other features that don't apply to Redstone builds that we won't get into here (like creating air right around them, which is useful for underwater building), but all you really need to know about Doors and Redstone is that they will open when powered.

Common Uses: Mostly as doors. So when in a Redstone build, it's usually just as part of a set up to open the Door, often by a Lever or Button or Pressure Plate.

Dispenser ✪✪✪

Primary Feature: Stores up to 9 stacks of items and "dispenses" one random item per 2 ticks (0.2 seconds) when powered unless the power stops. How the dispensing works depends on the item, but it is usually just thrown from the Dispenser.

Powered by:
- Components adjacent, above, below or attached to the Dispenser
- Powered block adjacent, above or below
- Dust, Comparator or Repeater powered and facing in to the Dispenser

Description: The Dispenser is mostly used for killin'. Well, that's not entirely true. It's also used to put armor on, so you can protect yourself from killin' when you go killin', and also for Potion throwing, to make you faster and stronger at killin'. Okay, it also has the ability to throw any other stackable item, but mostly Dispensers are hooked up to Redstone and filled with Arrows, Fire Charges, Lava Buckets, Flint and Steel and other things dangerous to both mob and player alike.

The Items

Note that a Dispenser is treated as an opaque block, meaning that it acts according to the rules as such. For instance, power can activate it a full power signal, and Redstone Torches can be attached to the Dispenser itself, but won't power it if they are attached to it and not simply adjacent.

When powered, the Dispenser waits 1 tick and then randomly dispenses one item from within it. Some items and blocks have special actions when a Dispenser drops them. Here's a list of the items that aren't just thrown from a Dispenser but have a special action that they take when the Dispenser is powered:

Armor: Auto-equips on a player if they are within 1 block and have an empty slot for that type of armor

Arrow: Fired the direction that the Dispenser is facing in the same way that a Bow would fire

Boat: Placed in front of the Dispenser as if from the player's inventory, meaning it can be set into Water by the Dispenser

Bone Meal: If dispensed onto a plant that reacts to Bone Meal, will cause that plant to grow in the same way that placing Bone Meal from the inventory would

Bottle o' Enchanting/Egg/Snowball/Splash Potion: Throws the item at whatever is in front of the Dispenser as if thrown from the inventory. So, can hit a mob or player if aimed right

Bucket: Picks up Water or Lava in front of the Dispenser and puts it in the Bucket

Command Block: Placed like a block normally would be and is activated instantly

Fire Charge: Fires a fireball out of the Dispenser in the way that a Blaze would

Firework Rocket: Sets the Firework in front of the Dispenser and launches it

Flint and Steel: Acts like Flint and Steel used by the player, lighting the block it's facing on fire

Lava/Water Bucket: Pours out the Lava or Water Bucket in front of the Dispenser

Minecart (all types): Places the Minecart if there are Rails of any kind in front of the Dispenser. Will place directly onto the Rails

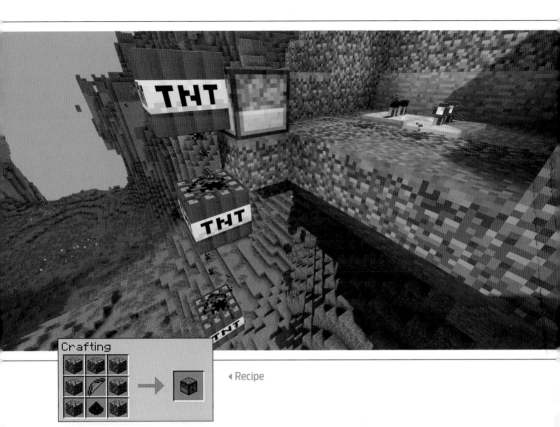

◄ Recipe

Mob Head/Pumpkin: Equipped instantly on a player within 1 block with an empty slot for head armor

Spawn Egg: Instantly spawns whatever mob that the egg is designated as

TNT: Drops the TNT down in front of the Dispenser and ignites it, and gives it a slight velocity to the explosion in a direction that is chosen randomly

Common Uses: Mostly used offensively or to equip armor/splash potions on a player quickly, but can also be set up in more complicated rigs to do things like dispense Water to harvest crops, create Lava traps for mobs and players or store and place multiple Minecarts quickly. Can get involved in more complex builds however, if, say, you were to use the Dispenser to place items on a Wooden Pressure Plate in certain circumstances, causing it to activate and send a power signal to a Redstone system. Can also fire Arrows at Wooden Buttons to activate them.

Piston/Sticky Piston ✪✪✪

Primary Feature: Pushes most blocks that are set in front of its "head (the side of the Piston that extends) when powered, but not all, will break most items, or will simply not extend into some other non-block entities as well as some blocks like Obsidian, other mechanisms, Chests, Beds and Signs (among others). Sticky Pistons will both push and retract a block in front of them (it is "stuck" to the Sticky Piston), and both regular and Sticky Pistons will push up to 12 blocks in a row (but no more per Piston, and only one drawn back with a Sticky Piston).

Powered by:
- Components adjacent, above or below
- Powered block adjacent, above or below
- Dust, Comparator or Repeater powered and facing in to the Piston or Sticky Piston
- Special powering note: Pistons can also be powered by a powered block one block above and one block to the side of the Piston, but this is a special kind of powering that will only cause the Piston to move when a "block update" happens.

Description: Pistons and Sticky Pistons are a very important component in many Redstone builds, including in those that do something mechanical (like harvesting plants), in some complex circuit builds, or those that include both.

For mechanical-type builds, the Piston/Sticky Piston's ability to push and/or pull blocks to shift blocks around for various reasons, including but (certainly) not limited to creating/closing openings (either to move through or for other reasons, like releasing Water or Lava) or breaking certain items and causing them to drop (like Wheat or even Redstone components themselves), is incredibly useful.

Circuit builds, on the other hand, that incorporate Pistons tend to have the Piston/Sticky Piston move a Block of Redstone, causing and/or breaking a connection, or they have the Pistons move blocks so that a circuit is broken otherwise. As an example of this last would be if a line of Redstone Dust travels up from one block to another one to the right and one up from the original block, raising the signal a level. If a Piston pushes a block two blocks above the original block, it will sit flush on one edge with the second Redstone-carrying block, and it will cut off the connection between that Redstone and that of the original block, killing the power signal.

The Items

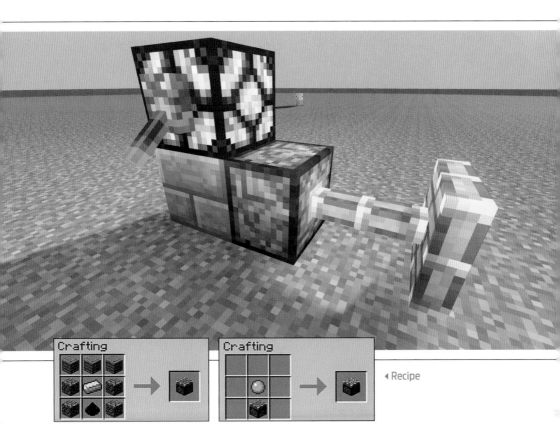

◀ Recipe

What is known as the "block update bug" gives Pistons the option to be activated by a powered block one block above and one block to the side of the Piston, which lets them be used in what is known as BUD switches, or Block Update Detectors, which essentially cause Redstone circuits to work based on these block updates instead of regular rules. Note: Pistons are not the only item that interacts with the block update detection bug, but it is one of the very most common to do so in useful ways. This is a complex concept, so don't worry too much about it here, but we'll talk a bit more about it in the Advanced Wiring chapter.

Pistons/Sticky Pistons and Slime Blocks also have a special relationship, which we'll talk more about in the Items entry for Slime Blocks in a few pages.

Common Uses: Fancy automatic doors (that don't use actual Doors), hidden bases and other toggle-able mechanical constructs like drawbridges, farming harvesters, traps, circuit components and even gates! Pistons are by far the most common and useful mechanism.

Fence Gates ⭐

Primary Feature: Opens in the same was as a Door or a Trapdoor when activated by a power signal. Provides an entrance that is only 1 block tall, otherwise does not do much with Redstone.

Powered by:

- Components adjacent, above or below
- Powered block adjacent, above or below
- Dust, Comparator or Repeater powered and facing in to the Fence Gate

◄ Recipe

Description: Fence Gates aren't too complex- if you know how a Door works, you know how a Fence Gate does. Basically all it does is open up when a power signal goes in. That's about it!

Common Uses: Mostly in house builds, such as to open a Fence Gate around a house, or in farming builds where pens of mobs are used.

Trapdoor ⭐

Primary Feature: Opens similarly to Doors and Fence Gates when activated by a Redstone signal. Can be useful in some odd Redstone builds for delaying floating or dropping items.

Powered by:
- Components adjacent
- Powered block adjacent, above or below
- Dust, Comparator or Repeater powered and facing in to the Trapdoor

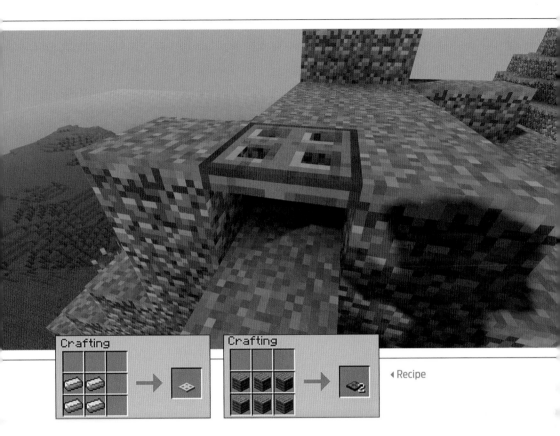

◀ Recipe

Description: These guys will open and close to any level of power like all other mechanisms. An open Trapdoor can block the space one block below where it is hanging, which is sometimes used in rare Redstone builds that have Boats or other things flowing through Water that need to be temporarily delayed. This also works in the opposite way for falling things like Minecarts or other items, as they will catch on a closed Trapdoor and then continue falling when it's opened. Like with Doors, Iron Trapdoors can only be opened with a Redstone signal, while Wooden can be opened by hand as well as by a signal. Not exactly a common thing to need in Redstone, but there are some creative things that can be done with them.

Common Uses: Mostly just as entrances, but can act as a temporary barrier as noted in the description.

Hopper ✪✪✪

Primary Feature: Sucks in one item every 4 ticks that is floating in the space one block immediately above it or from another container that the Hopper is below, and can spit one item at a time out into a container that it faces (an item exchange rate of 2.5 items a second). Can store five stacks of items in a mini-inventory when sucked in, or it will suck in one item and also push one item from its inventory to a container.

Description: The Hopper acts as a small container as well as a mechanism that can shift items either from the space above it, or from a container, to its own inventory or to other containers (including other Hoppers, which is called a "Hopper pipe"). If the Hopper is hooked up to a container, the items sucked in will always go to the attached container instead of staying in the Hopper's inventory, and the items will always be transferred one at a time starting with the item that was most recently sucked up by the Hopper.

A particularity of Hoppers is that unlike all other mechanisms, they are automatically on. A Redstone signal, then will turn off, or "disable" the Hopper, instead of turning it on. This is technically still activating the mechanism, though it acts in reverse of most others.

The Items

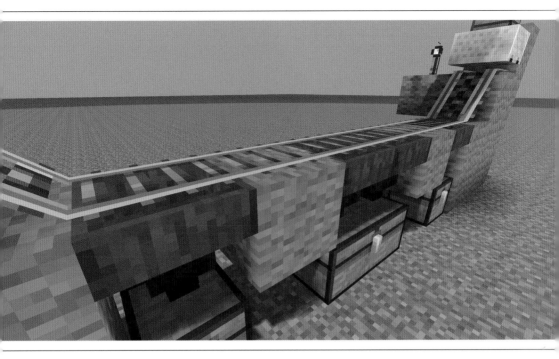

Hoppers that float free of other containers will just take items into their inventory and not push them out, and they can only hold a max of five stacks of items. It should be noted that items will still only stack with items of the same kind, meaning you can actually only have a maximum of five types of items in a Hopper, regardless of how many of each of those items it contains.

This ability to shift items around makes the Hopper very important to automation (see the Automation chapter for more on this), as it allows items to be automatically transferred to various containers (even allowing for auto-sorting of items) as well as to crafting items like Furnaces and Brewing Stands. Players often hook up Hoppers to Rail systems that use Minecarts with Chests to either auto-sort items into stationary Chests by item type or to automate the creation of items in things like the Furnace, as the Hopper can pull items from a Minecart with Chest that passes over the Hopper.

Hoppers can be hooked up to various sides of certain items in order to produce different results. To set a Hopper on a certain side of an item like a Furnace, you'll need to set the Furnace down, select the Hopper in your item tray, and then shift as you click on the Furnace.

Here is a very basic rundown of what various items Hoppers can be hooked up to, and any special notes about how the combination works:

Brewing Stand: Can cause auto-brewing of Potions by placing Hoppers that contain or pull brewing ingredients if attached to the right place on the Brewing Stand. Hoppers placed above will fill the top Brewing Stand slot, Hoppers to the side will fill the bottom three Brewing Stand slots, and Hoppers below will pull from the Potion slot, though it will not automatically wait for the Potion to be done to pull it out.

Chest/Trapped Chest: Will fill from left to right, and only one Hopper is needed to fill double Chests. If you open a Trapped Chest with a Hopper attached, it will send a Redstone signal out that will stop the Hopper until you close the chest.

Dispenser/Dropper: Fills left to right

Furnace: Hopper above will fill the ingredient slot, Hopper to the side will fill the fuel slot, Hopper below will pull from the "cooked" (aka output) slot.

Crafting

◀ Recipe

Hopper(s): Will pull an item from the Hopper ahead/above it in the "pipe," and will also push the item to the next Hopper in the pipe if there is one. Vertical Hopper pipes will move items twice as fast, as the item is both being pulled by the new Hopper and "pushed" out by the former Hopper at the same time. Only one Hopper in the pipe needs to be disabled to stop the pipe entirely in horizontal pipes, while two need to be disabled in a vertical pipe.

Minecart with Chest/Minecart with Hopper: Will push items into Minecarts with Chests/Hoppers if facing toward it (whether from the side or above), and will pull from below them. Note that this will not work when there is a Detector Rail above the Hopper, because the signal from the Detector Rail will disable the Hopper.

Ender Chest: Does not work with Hoppers.

Common Uses: Typically for automation or storage builds, making large-scale storing or creation of certain items much quicker to complete, if much more complicated to set up.

Other Recipes Used In: Minecart with Hopper

Dropper ✪✪

Primary Feature: "Drops" items when activated, which is different from a Dispenser in that it will always drop items as an entity instead of in a special way (such as firing Arrows or Fire Charges, or dumping Water or Lava Buckets), and Droppers will also push items from their inventory into a container if they are facing one.

Powered by:

- Components adjacent, above, below or attached to the Dropper
- Powered block adjacent, above or below
- Dust, Comparator or Repeater powered and facing in to the Dropper

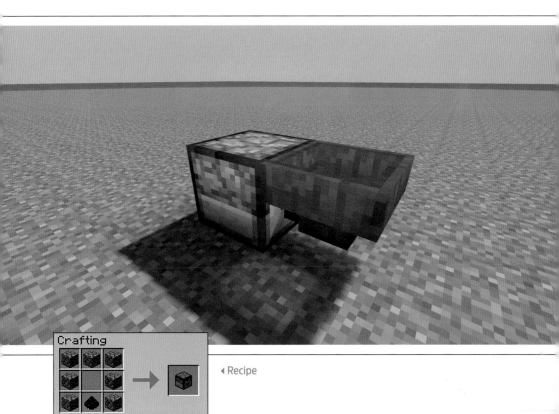

Crafting

◀ Recipe

Description: Droppers are a fairly new mechanism compared to Dispensers, and they are essentially the exact same thing except that they will always throw items that they hold as an actual item entity instead of in any special way. Droppers also have the extra ability to push items that they hold into other containers that they are facing, including Chests, another Dropper, Hoppers or a Dispenser.

Common Uses: Where a Dispenser would be used, but you want the items inside to only be dropped as an item entity, or to be put into a container.

Rails that Interact with Redstone

Rails and Redstone are very closely intertwined, as much of what Rail systems can do requires Redstone to work. On the other hand, however, some Rails can actually be integral parts of both the mechanical and the power side of many types of Redstone builds.

Detector Rail ✪✪✪

Primary Feature: When a Minecart of any kind runs over the Detector Rail, it puts out a full power signal. If the Minecart has a Chest, Comparators hooked up to the Detector Rail will put out an output level based on the amount of items in the container, as it would with a non-mobile chest, but temporarily.

Powers:
- Block it's on (if opaque)
- Dust adjacent
- Repeaters and Comparators adjacent and facing away from the Detector Rail
- Mechanisms adjacent, above or below

The Items

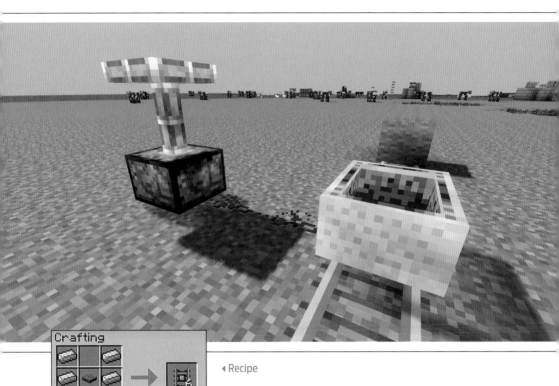

Crafting

◄ Recipe

Description: Essentially a button activated by a Minecart, Detector Rails give a full signal while a Minecart is on them, and then the signal stops when the Minecart moves off of it. Their ability to power Comparators at variable levels when they interact with Minecarts with Chests is also quite useful.

Common Uses: Somewhat common in Redstone builds that use Rails of any kind, like roller coasters and the like, but also sometimes used in special kinds of manually built repeaters (using Powered Rails, one can set up a system where Minecarts run over a Detector Rail every so often). Also in builds with Comparators in order to achieve temporary signals of varying strength.

Activator Rail ✪✪

Primary Feature: Activates certain features of the normal, Command Block, Hopper and TNT variatons of Minecarts when they run over a powered Activator Rail.

Powered by:
- Components adjacent
- Powered block adjacent
- Dust, Comparator or Repeater powered and facing in to the Activator Rail

Description: Activator Rails act on Minecarts, and they can also activate other adjacent Activator Rails, but that's about all they do. When it comes to Minecarts, the interaction depends on the type of cart, as seen here:

Regular Minecart: Ejects mobs and players from the Minecart

Hopper Minecart: Turns off the Hopper if Activator Rail is activated, turns on if Activator Rail is deactivated

The Items

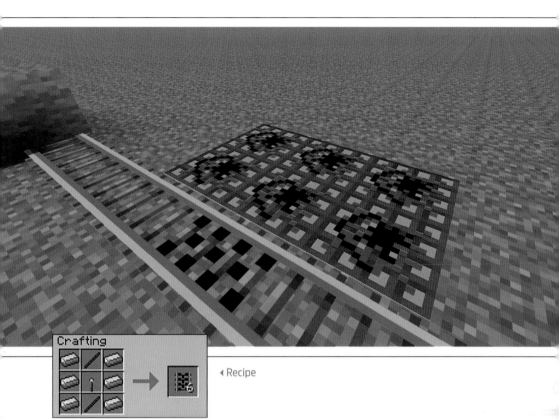

◄ Recipe

Command Block Minecart: Activates the Command Block for as long as the Minecart is on the Activator Rail

TNT Minecart: Sets this baby off! Technically it starts the ignition process, exploding one second later. A cool feature is that the level of explosion will be proportional to the Minecart's speed as it passes over the Activator. So get those things goin' fast, and you'll get one big boom.

Common Uses: Specialty builds, usually just to create a specific situation in a Rail system, such as auto-clearing mobs from Minecarts.

Recipe ▶

Powered Rail ✪✪✪

Primary Feature: Provides a boost of speed to Minecarts that pass over it when the Powered Rail is actually powered by a power component. Will slow a Minecart if unpowered.

Powered by:
- Components adjacent
- Powered block adjacent
- Dust, Comparator or Repeater powered and facing in to the Powered Rail

Description: Basically these guys are used to drive Minecarts along a Rail system so that the carts move (and also to stop) without someone having to physically push them. They can be powered by sources adjacent, and they can also power other adjacent Powered Rails (up to 17 Powered Rails).

Common Uses: Not much as an actual Redstone component that interacts with others, but almost always used in any kind of Rail system, including those that have other Redstone features.

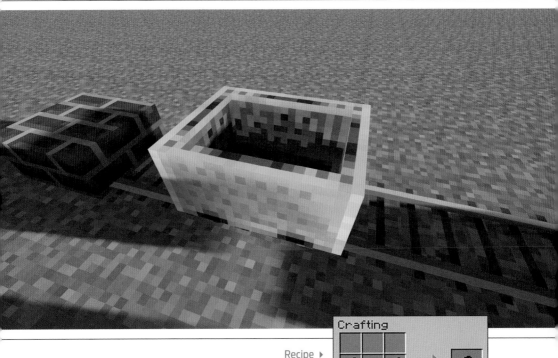

Recipe ▶

Minecart ✪✪✪

Primary Feature: Concerning Redstone, the primary feature is to interact with the different types of Rails that use Redstone, most especially the Detector Rail, which combines with the Minecart to make a source of power.

Description: As said above, the Minecart's importance to Redstone is primarily in relation to the types of Redstone Rails that exist. It is necessary to have a Minecart roll over both the Detector Rail and the Activator Rail in order to make them function, and it also is what the Powered Rail acts on.

Common Uses: When Detector Rails and the power signal they produce are important to a build, otherwise just in general Rail builds. One complex way to use Minecarts with Redstone is to use Detector Rails with Comparators and Minecarts with Chests, having the Comparator read the amount of items in each Chest and putting out customizable levels of usable power signals.

Other Recipes Used In: Minecart with Chest, Minecart with Furnace, Minecart with Hopper, Minecart with TNT

Other Items that Interact with Redstone

Mostly just fun novelties, these guys take Redstone signals to perform their action, but they aren't mechanical and don't really fit in elsewhere. One-offs, but fun!

Note Block ✪

Primary Feature: Makes a customizable noise when activated with a power source.

Powered by:
- Components adjacent, above or below
- Powered block adjacent, above or below
- Dust, Comparator or Repeater powered and facing in to the Note Block

◀ Recipe

Description: Note Blocks are just a fun little item that has no other use than to make noise when activated by Redstone power. You can set the note you want the Note Block to play with right clicking, and they need an empty block above them to play. They can be powered with a Lever on them, but the Lever sound is almost louder than the note, and they can't be powered by something above them, because they need that block empty to play.

Common Uses: Doorbells and other times you'd like Minecraft to make noise. Some people have created entire songs using many Note Blocks set on Repeater delays.

Recipe ▸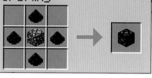

Redstone Lamp ✪✪

Primary Feature: Acts as a light source instantly when powered by Redstone.

Powered by:

- Components adjacent, above or below
- Powered block adjacent, above or below
- Dust, Comparator or Repeater powered and facing in to the Redstone Lamp

Description: Redstone Lamps are the fanciest of Minecraft light sources, in that they are not small Torches or natural Glowstone and they require Redstone power to work. They'll put out a source of light instantly that is 15, the highest light value in the game, and they'll turn off when unpowered, though it takes 2 ticks to shut off.

Common Uses: Just to light up the land, really. It's simply another way to do lighting, giving you the option to be more creative with it as it can be turned on and off at whim. You can even rig Redstone Lamps up to flash, but you have to make sure to account for the 2 tick delay on shutting down, or they'll just stay on.

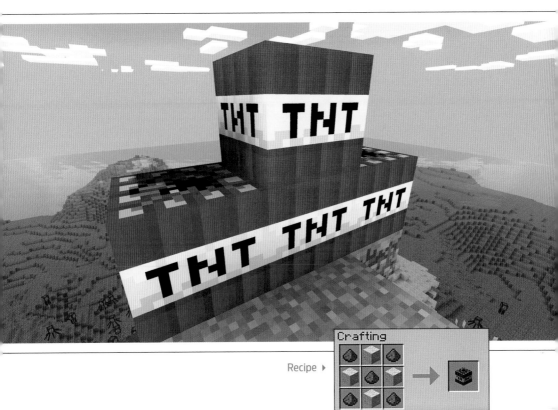

Recipe ▸

TNT ✪✪

Primary Feature: Ignites when activated, which can be done with a Redstone signal, and when ignited this way (or by fire) its 'fuse' lasts 40 ticks.

Powered by:
- Components adjacent, above or below
- Powered block adjacent, above or below
- Dust, Comparator or Repeater powered and facing in to TNT

Description: TNT is the biggest destructive force in vanilla Minecraft, and its use as a Redstone component mostly deals with using Redstone to ignite the stuff. This is useful for safely blowin' the crap out of large areas by creating a line of Redstone from a TNT stack to a power component (think like the oldschool 'line of gunpowder leading to the pile of dynamite' trope), but it's also used to create cannons and TNT traps, which themselves are usually powered by Redstone at some point. TNT doesn't otherwise interact with Redstone much.

Common Uses: Mostly just 'splodey stuff, but particularly traps and cannons. Check out the Intermediate Builds section for how to make a real nice TNT cannon.

Other Recipes Used In: Minecart with TNT

Water/Lava ⊙⊙

Primary Feature: Breaks a Redstone connection by pouring through the space where part of a Redstone component exists. Can also be used as part of a mechanism, such as by using a Dispenser to pick up or drop a bucket of either, or in special builds where things moving through Water are necessary.

Description: Water and Lava aren't very big parts of most Redstone machines, but they can be useful in very special situations. For instance, you could use either as a self-destruct system for your Redstone build, or even just part of it (whether for fun or practicality). Some complex systems use Water to move things along, either in order to gather them (like in a plant-harvesting water scythe), or to move things to where they can then fall to activate a Pressure Plate (complex, but possible).

Common Uses: Mostly for destruction of a Redstone build or in builds that utilize Water.

Basic Blocks and Redstone

Beyond the opaque block that we've mentioned many times already, a few other block-types have particular interactions with Redstone, most of which are very important.

Slabs ✪✪✪

Primary Feature: Allow Redstone signals to be transmitted upwards due to the property of Slabs that allows Redstone to be placed on the top of a Slab, but only on ones set in the top half of a block space (called an upside down Slab). Redstone cannot be placed on Slabs placed on the bottom half of a block space. They do not cut off a signal when placed caddy-corner to each other, unlike how it works with regular blocks.

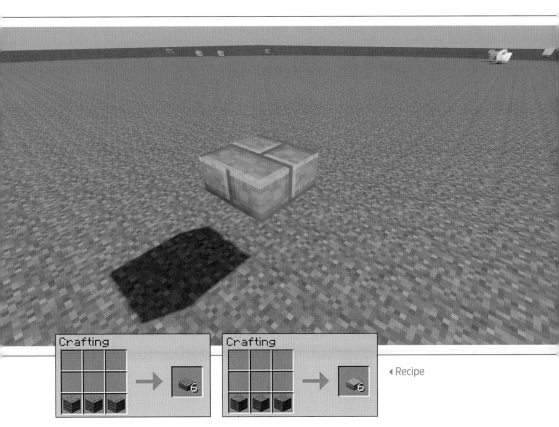

◄ Recipe

Description: Slabs have one use with Redstone, but it's a biggie: they are used in one of the most common Redstone transmission builds called a "ladder," which is a construct that transmits a Redstone signal upwards in a compact way (without using the "staircase" method, more on ladders and staircasing in the Advanced Wiring chapter). Other than that, they're not used for most Redstoning purposes, but ladders are very important, making Slabs a commonly-used block in big Redstone builds.

Common Uses: Redstone ladders, for the most part.

Other Recipes Used In: Armor Stand, Chiseled Blocks (Quartz, Red Sandstone, Sandstone, Stone Brick), Daylight Sensor

Transparent Blocks ✪✪✪

Primary Feature: Used in Redstone ladders and diodes (basically a one-step ladder meant to use the feature that a Redstone signal can move up a ladder but not down it, but not specifically to transmit the signal a large distance upwards like the ladder), there are various "transparent" blocks on which Redstone can be placed. The "transparent"-ness of these blocks allows them to be placed in a way so that they propagate a signal one block upwards while only needing a build 2 blocks wide, 2 blocks tall and 1 block deep to do so.

Description: Transparent blocks are very important in Redstone specifically because some of them are able to be used to transmit a Redstone signal vertically in a very compact manner and without necessarily using any Redstone Torches. Not all transparent blocks have this feature, but the following blocks (excluding slabs, which work with ladders and can be read about in the previous entry) will work in a Redstone ladder:

- Glowstone
- Upside-down Stairs

Common Uses: As ladder components, but they can of course be used in other parts of a build, just not typically as a Redstone component.

Slime Block ⊘⊘

Primary Feature: Interacts in special ways with other game elements, especially Pistons (when talking about Redstone). Will "bounce" players, mobs and gravity blocks (like Sand or Anvils) to a height that gets greater with higher velocity when hitting the Slime Block, which can be used as the goal of some Redstone builds. Slime Blocks can have Redstone components placed on them (this will not cancel out the bouncing feature of the Slime Block), and they can even be powered by Redstone like an opaque block. Concerning Pistons, Slime Blocks on the end of a Piston or Sticky Piston will attempt to move any adjacent blocks that would normally be moved by a Piston (meaning those that are not immovable blocks or blocks that would have to be pushed "through" an immovable block), which may in turn move other blocks if there is a movable block in the path of the block moved by the Slime Block and Piston, up to 12 blocks. Entities in the path of a Slime Block that's moved by a Piston will also be launched in the direction the Piston is moving in.

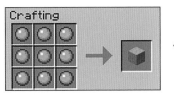

◄ Recipe

Description: A fairly recent addition to Minecraft, the Slime Block is a quirky green block made from Slimeballs whose primary features are its bounciness and, more importantly to Redstone, its use with Pistons. As seen in the Primary Feature section, Slime Blocks attached to Pistons will push up to 12 other blocks along with the Slime Block if they are adjacent to the Slime Block and are movable, or if they are movable and in the path of another block moved by the Slime Block. This feature further applies to Slime Blocks themselves, as up to 12 adjacent Slime Blocks will both push and pull together meaning a chunk of Slime Blocks put together can be moved by Pistons as a unit by acting on only one block. They can even push out blocks of other kinds at the end of their own line, if the number is still 12 or less total blocks (including the Slime Blocks).

This feature of moving other blocks and other Slime Blocks has allowed creators to do something that was nearly impossible before without mods, which is to create self-propelled constructs. Using a series of Pistons, Slime Blocks and power components in the right way, players can create machines that will slowly move across the ground or sky one block at a time, which is both very fun and also somewhat complex to do (see Advanced Builds for more on how to build one of these bad boys!).

Common Uses: Anything where shifting large amounts of blocks around would be useful (can be used to close and break circuits by shifting over Redstone Dust and other powered components), but the most popular use as of yet has been to make flying and crawling machines with Slime Blocks. Also can make a few types of "cannons" (TNT, Fire Charges and others), Piston doors, elevators and much more.

Other Recipes Used In: Can be turned back into 9 Slimeballs

Your First 5
Redstone Builds

All this talk about the components and concepts and rules of Redstone has probably got you a bit overwhelmed, but don't worry: actually doing a little Redstone will help you tremendously in figuring out just what all that information means, as well as how to use it to make MInecraft even more awesome than it already is.

So, young crafters, here's the part where we stop just telling you about Redstone and start actually makin' some cool stuff! These are your first five true Redstone builds, starting from the simplest Redstone doorbell and going through an awesome-lookin' Piston wave that's a great and easy way to impress those who don't have your Redstone skills.

These builds are designed to be super simple to build, in order to get you comfortable with using Redstone, yet they'll also teach you important lessons about Redstone and its properties. The builds also incorporate a few more complex properties and functions of Redstone, such as a NOT Gate and a clock, which you'll become much more familiar with later in the book as we get into more complex and difficult Redstone builds.

For now, however, we just want to focus on building the five contraptions here and understanding the simple basics of how they work. Later, we'll get into the more complex ideas behind some of the functions in these builds, but this chapter is all about dipping your toes into the world of Redstone in the simplest, most pain-free way possible. All you've got to do is follow the instructions and then recreate what you see in the images, and you'll already be on your way to earning your honorary Master's degree in Redstone Engineering.

Note: We recommend doing this in Creative Mode in order to learn these builds, but you can do them in Survival Mode as well if you have the materials.

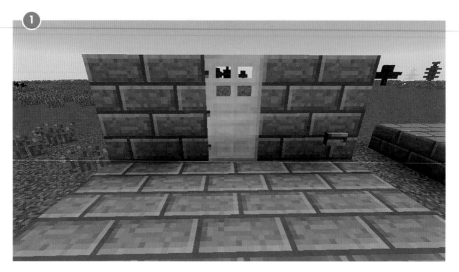

The Doorbell

What it does: Lets ya know someone wants in your house by making a ding (or y'know, whatever weird noise you set it to).

How it works: A Note Block inside your home makes a noise when someone outside pushes a Button, powering the Note Block.

You'll Need: 1 Button, 1 Note Block, Redstone (optional)

Makin' a working, useful doorbell is just about the easiest Redstone project you'll ever do. In fact, it can be done without any Redstone Wire at all if you don't mind the Note Block being right inside your door. This is a good project to just get an idea of how power-giving items

such as Buttons work with items like the Note Block that take power, and it's a cute little way to spruce up your home. Plus, Note Blocks can be heard up to 48 blocks from its location, so it will inform you of visitors even at a good distance.

1. Find the spot where you'd like to put the button that will activate your doorbell. Typically these are placed by a Door, but you could do it anywhere you wanted. For the easiest Doorbell, pick a spot on a wall near a Door that is one block off the ground and where the wall is just one block thick behind where the Button will be. Place the Button on this block.

2. Place the Note Block on the other side of the block that now has a Button on it.

3. If the block under the Note Block is one you placed yourself, break it and leave the space empty. If you can't remember if you placed the block then go ahead and break it. This is done because the Note Block will change to a different sound than the beep we want if a human-placed block is underneath it.

4. Right-click the Note Block until it hits the note you'd like to use as your doorbell. This can be a little tricky, as sometimes the Note Block doesn't want to make noise, but just break the block and put it back down if you can't get it to work at first.

5. Press the Button back on the other side of the wall, and the Note Block will make its sound! The way this works is that the Button gives power to the block it is placed on, and this block gives power to the Note Block.

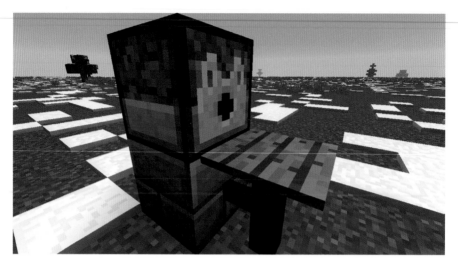

The Easy Potion Dispenser

What it does: Throws a Potion out at you when you run up and bump it (no need to click on this one).

How it works: A Dispenser is placed on a block, a Fence is placed in front of the block and Dispenser, and on top of the Fence is a Pressure Plate. When you run up to the Pressure Plate and push your crafter into it, it will press down, and whatever is in the Dispenser will launch out (Potions, in this case)

You'll Need: 1 Dispenser, 1 Fence, 1 Pressure Plate, 1 random block (optional, Dispenser could hang in the air), whatever Potions you want to dispense

Your First 5 Redstone Builds

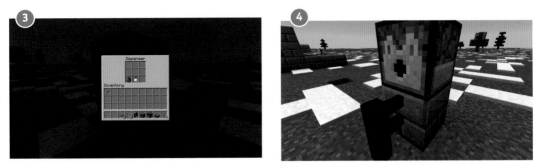

Another quite simple little doohickey, the easy Potion dispenser makes taking Potions in Minecraft about as easy as it can be. Typically, you have to open your inventory or go to your hot bar and actually use a potion, or even run up to a Dispenser and push a Button or pull a Lever to get one to launch out at you. However, with the Easy Potion Dispenser, all you have to do is run up and bump the Pressure Plate, and you'll be smartly splashed with Potion.

1. Place a block of any kind down.

2. Put a Dispenser on top of this block.

3. Fill the Dispenser with a Potion of your choosing. This will actually work with anything a Dispenser can dispense at you, but Potions are one of the most useful options in this configuration.

4. Stand so the Dispenser is facing you (the side with the O-shaped hole) and look down at the block it is sitting on. Place one Fence on the block that is in front of this block that the Dispenser is on.

5. Place a Pressure Plate on top of the one Fence you have just placed.

6. Run up to the Pressure Plate, and it will press down and the Potion (or whatever else you've got in the Dispenser) will launch out. This is the Pressure Plate activating from interacting with your body and powering the Dispenser, which fires a random item inside of it at you.

The Trapdoor

What it does: Opens a hole in the ground wherever you'd like (in this case in front of a Door) at the flick of a Lever. Beneath this hole that opens is a big pit and/or Lava, which anything that was standing on the block above the hole will fall into.

How it works: A Sticky Piston is attached to a block and extended over a pit, covering the hole. The Sticky Piston is attached underground to a Redstone "gate" called a NOT Gate (look to the Gates chapter for further explanation of this), which goes beneath the wall of a house using Redstone Wire. On the other side of the wall, a Lever on the ground surface turns the signal for the Redstone wire on and off, causing the Sticky Piston to expose and to cover the pit, alternatively. The whole contraption is hidden.

You'll Need: 1 Sticky Piston, 1 Lever, 1 Redstone Torch, 2 Redstone Wire, 2 Slabs of any kind, 1 random block

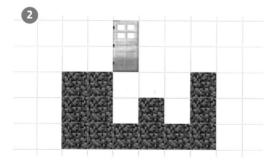

Diagram designed at mordritch.com

Your First 5 Redstone Builds

1. Find yourself a nice Door. This Door should be one which you would like to look out of, see a Creeper, and then kill that Creeper by making it drop to its doom. Also works with annoying players.

2. Dig out a pit in the pattern of Diagram 1. It should be only 1 block wide and 3 long, and it should alternate being 2 and 1 and then 2 blocks deep, as you also see in the Diagram.

3. Place a Redstone Torch on the wall as you see in the photo here.

4. Put a Sticky Piston in the space above the Redstone Torch facing toward the space in front of the Door (it will extend automatically), and then put a block of whatever type you'd like in front of the Sticky Piston. The 1 block deep hole in front of the Door should now be covered by the block stuck to the Sticky Piston.

5. Go to the other side of the wall which the Door is set in. Dig out a pit immediately on the other side of the wall from the block where the Sticky Piston and Redstone Torch are. Make this pit 1 block wide, 2 blocks long and 2 blocks deep.

6. Lay Redstone Wire down on the bottom of this pit. This is not essential to understand at this point, but what you have created in this section of the build is represented in the Diagram.

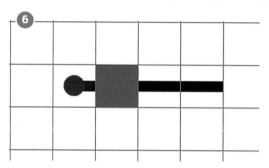

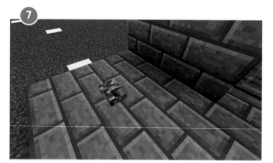

Diagram designed at mordritch.com

By adding a power source to the end of the Redstone Wire in the Diagram (or on a block above it, as we will do in the next step), we create what is called a NOT Gate. A NOT Gate is a type of construction known as a logic gate, which manipulates a Redstone signal and is something we will learn in the future chapter on Gates.

7. Cover the last block of the pit (farthest from the wall) with the same type of block that makes up the rest of the floor. Put a Lever on top of this block. Now cover the second block of the pit with the same type of block, but with no Lever.

8. Flip the Lever and the Sticky Piston should pull back and uncover the hole in front of the Door.

9. Go back through the Door to the pit in front of it, and dig the pit deeper. Here you have a few options: place Lava or Cactus at the bottom of the pit to kill intruders with damage, make a long drop that will kill the intruder (at least 24 blocks down for a TKO), or build an area at the bottom for the intruders to fall into and just, y'know, hang out. Until you come to slice them up with your Sword, of course.

10. Go back up and cover up the Sticky Piston by placing 2 Slabs of any kind on top of the two blocks it takes up. Don't put one over the spot in front of the door, of course.

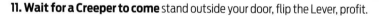

11. Wait for a Creeper to come stand outside your door, flip the Lever, profit.

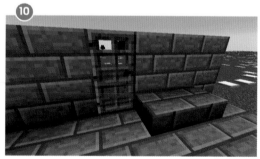

The Simplest Clock

What it does: Creates a pulse of Redstone power that turns on and off at a regular interval, which allows many concepts to be created with Redstone, including but not limited to contraptions that keep time.

How it works: A Redstone Torch powers a Redstone Repeater, which slows down the signal slightly (in this case it is a '4 tick' delay). After 4 ticks the power goes through the Repeater and on to the Wire after it, which curves around to power the block that the original Redstone Torch was on. This turns off the Redstone Torch temporarily, in turn turning off the signal through the Redstone Repeater after 4 more ticks. This repeats indefinitely unless acted upon from an outside signal.

You'll Need: 1 Redstone Torch, 1 Redstone Repeater, 3 Redstone Wire, 1 Random Block

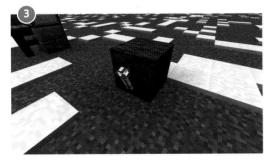

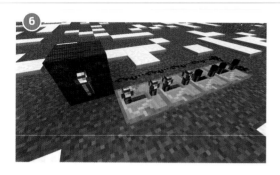

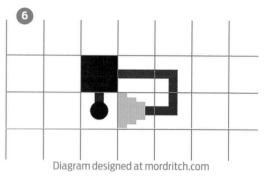

Diagram designed at mordritch.com

When referring to Redstone components, a "clock" is a Redstone construction that alternately causes an on signal and then an off signal to be transmitted from itself every so many seconds in a constant pulse.

Clocks are power loops, where a signal is transmitted from a power source, slowed down by Repeaters (or other ways, in more complex cases), and then is sent back to the original power source, temporarily turning it off. This causes the power to pulse with a consistent amount of time between each pulse, and the amount of time between each pulse can be customized by the builder through using multiple Repeaters in a row as well as other tactics.

This pulsing signal can be used to give something else power for a few ticks, and then take it away. So for instance, a Piston hooked up to a clock would continuously extend and pull back as long as it was hooked up to the clock.

This is the simplest version of a clock, and it's quite useful for everything from practical, mechanical Redstone builds to the most complex logic circuits.

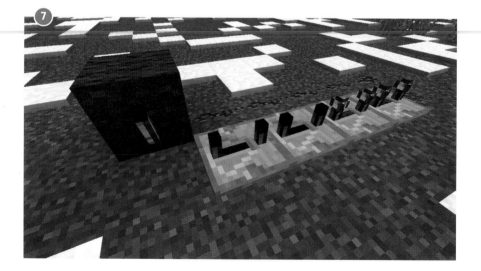

Your First 5 Redstone Builds

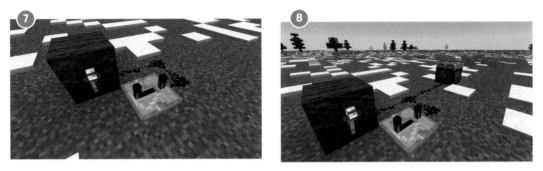

1. Turn so that the direction you would like your power to go in is to your right. Make sure there are about five blocks of usable ground space to your right (if there is not, scooch over a bit so there is).

2. Place your random block down. This has to be one that can transfer power, so something like Stone, Wool or Wood of any type is good.

3. Keeping the direction you would like the signal to move in to your right, place a Redstone Torch on the side of the block facing you, as in the image.

4. As in the image, place a Redstone Repeater on the block to the right of the block that your Redstone Torch hangs over (so, caddy-corner to the block the Redstone Torch is on).

5. Set this repeater on the last setting (4 ticks). This is important- Redstone Torches cannot take a signal that is too fast coming back into them, and Redstone Torches will burn out after a while if you have too quick of a signal piping into them (turn your Repeater to a faster signal when your clock is fully built and test it out sometime, just to see this happen). The reason for this is somewhat complex, but all you need to know at this point is that you need to slow this signal down a bit with your Repeater.

6. Copy the Redstone pattern from the Diagram, taking it one block on the ground past the repeater, then both blocks on the ground to the right of the block you have a Torch on.

7. If you have set the Repeater to the right delay in step #5, your clock will start working immediately, doing a pulsing signal.

8. To use your clock, just put 1 Redstone Wire branching off the existing Redstone Wire in the clock. You can then extend this to whatever you want to power.

Tips: You can put a Lever on the side of the block in your Redstone clock, and you can turn the clock on and off with the Lever.

You can create clocks with greater delays (much greater, theoretically) by using more Redstone Repeaters in a row.

The Piston Wave

What it does: Causes a series of Pistons (or Sticky Pistons) to extend and pull back with each consecutive Piston firing slightly after the last, making a visual wave.

How it works: A clock (see previous First Build section for how to build) powers a series of Redstone Wires in which there is a Redstone Repeater set every other block. The Repeaters are all set to the same delay (does not matter how long), and a signal branches off from the main Redstone Wire directly after each Repeater to a Piston. This makes each Piston fire, and since the signal is delayed by each subsequent Repeater, each Piston fires slightly after the last. The Pistons also immediately retract as the signal from the clock comes in a pulse and is not constant.

You'll Need: 8 Pistons (or Sticky Pistons), 27 Redstone, 8 Redstone Repeaters, 1 Redstone Torch, 1 Random block.

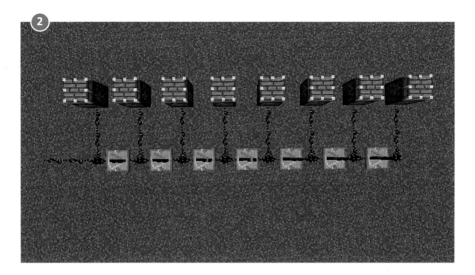

This build really doesn't do much that is practical, but it's fun to see and helps to visualize the effect of Redstone Repeaters on a signal. It combines a few very simple Redstone concepts that have been approached in the previous builds in this section in a fun way that makes a sweet visual Piston wave, and it doesn't take much to build. This construct could be applied to some visual effects you might want to create in complex Redstone maps, but for the most part it is useful simply for the way it demonstrates what a pulsing signal and a signal slowed by Repeaters can both do.

1. Build a clock using the instructions in the previous build. Make sure the out signal from the clock faces where you'd like your line of firing Pistons to be.

2. Attached to the Wire coming out of the clock, put a Redstone Wire, then a Redstone Repeater, and then another Redstone Wire and another Redstone Repeater (make sure that the Repeaters are facing the right way so that the signal continues to the next Wire). Keep

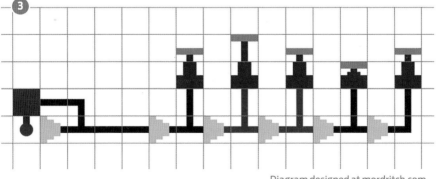

Diagram designed at mordritch.com

doing this until you have placed down the 7 remaining Redstone Repeaters (after using 1 for the clock). It should be a line of alternating Wires and Repeaters attached to the clock, and if the clock is on (as in the Wire has not been broken or it has not been turned off with a Lever), you will see the signal pulse through the Redstone Wire and Repeaters one by one. Put each Repeater on the same delay at first (though it doesn't matter which particular tick you set them on, as long as they're all the same), and, if you want, you can go in later and tweak it however you like to test what it does to the wave.

3. Place more Redstone down, this time placing 2 Redstone Wire off each Redstone Wire to the left of every Redstone Repeater you have placed (except, of course, the one in your clock). Also place 2 coming off to the right of the final Repeater. Make sure all wires go in the same direction. Refer to the image to see exactly how to do this.

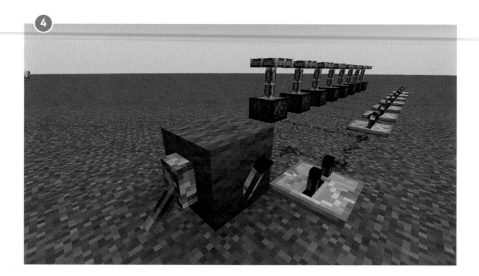

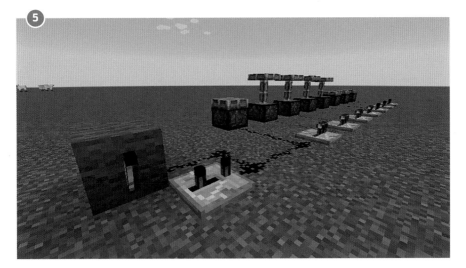

4. Place a Piston facing straight up to the sky at the end of each of these branches of Redstone Wire that you have just created. Note: you may want to turn off the clock while you do this, as when all the Pistons fire it will make a lot of noise until you turn it off. It can get super annoying.

5. When wired up to the clock (and with the clock on), the signal will proliferate through the Wire and each Repeater in turn, taking a few ticks each time before it goes through to the next set of Wires and Repeater. This will cause the signal that goes out to each Piston to come a little behind the signal to the Piston to its left, and the Pistons will fire in a wave. Use this construct to observe how signals can be delayed, and play around with the time that each Repeater is set to in order to get an even better sense of the way time works with Redstone. You can also make this build look a little cooler by doing things like using Sticky Pistons with Glowstone attached instead of regular Pistons.

Redstone **Gates**
What They Are and Why You Need to Know 'Em

Ready to have your brain busted? Well, unless you've already got a good bit of learnin' accomplished in the fields of logic or computer programming/building (and we don't mean installing more memory into your PC, we mean the actual construction of those memory chips), chances are this section of our little guide is going to be a bit of a noggin'-expander. But don't get your head all worried- we mean that in a good way!

What we're tackling in this chapter are the ever-important, all-powerful Redstone gates. These little constructs are simple to build, yet are the hardest part of Redstone to master, and in the end they're what allow most every Redstone build to work. They can be used in everything from a simple mob detection system (which uses a basic NOT gate or so), to the most mind-bogglingly complex Redstone computers that need an engineering degree to understand and build (and which use just about every single version of these gates that there is, and thousands of each).

So what the heck are Redstone gates?

The Deep Explanation

Well, this is actually quite a complex subject, especially for a video game. To start with, know that it's not necessary to grasp the entirety of this concept right now as you read through this chapter. Like much of this book, the important part here is just to read the words over so that you get familiar with the ideas, and then to try and recreate the gates you see in the pictures so that you start using them yourself. Redstone gates are fascinating and are worth learning not only to get better at building in Minecraft, but also because even attempting to understand gates will make you smarter and will help you to learn how actual real-life things like computers and electronics function (which might even help you in a future job!).

But, even some very highly educated people struggle with these concepts, so don't worry about trying to understand the whole thing all at once. Understanding will come with time and practice, and besides, there's always something more to be learned about Redstone gates once you get the hang of all of this you see here.

To get on the right track and to start to understand what Redstone gates are, let's begin with two ideas:

1. Redstone gates are circuits built out of Redstone, very similar to the kind of circuits that make up the wiring in everything electronic in your home, from the somewhat simple wiring that goes through your home to all of its lights, to the incredibly complex wiring that makes up the circuits of the computer or console on which you play Minecraft. Redstone gates, like those circuits, take power signals and combine and manipulate these signals in order to achieve a specific result. For lights, this result means turning on. For Redstone gates, it can mean a variety of things, from causing a Piston to activate to powering the input to yet another Redstone gate.

This works like this: each gate (and each circuit in your electronics) takes these input signals and reads what they are, and then manipulates them based on how the gate (or circuit) is built, and then the gate (or circuit) outputs a new signal based on that manipulation. For real circuits, these outputs have a lot of variety, but for Minecraft's purposes, the output is either ON or OFF. This concept of ON or OFF leads us to our second idea for understanding Redstone gates.

2. Redstone gates are a way to create what are known in the world outside of Minecraft as "logic gates," except you build them in the game. Though Redstone gates are often called circuits, and are very similar to electronic circuitry, it is actually a bit more useful and more apt to compare Redstone gates to the field of logic than to electronics. In logic, various combinations of ON inputs (also sometimes known as 1, A, or HIGH inputs) and OFF inputs (also known as 0, B, or LOW inputs) go into mental constructs known as logic gates that function in much the same way that Redstone gates do, except instead of having "physical" parts like Redstone Torches and Dust and blocks creating the gate (or real physical parts like actual wires, for electronic gates), the gate is all in the mind.

This may make Redstone gates seem more similar to electronic gates than logic gates, since they both require actual construction, but the truth is that electronics feature a lot more special "rules" than Redstone does, which have to do with the physical properties of wires and electricity. Redstone, on the other hand, is created in a virtual world with far fewer rules and restrictions, and which can be referred to as a simulation. Since creating and using logic gates inside your mind by thinking of them can also be thought of as a simulation, you can start to see why logic gates and Redstone gates have a lot in common.

What It Means for Minecraft

In the end, all this fancy talk and high theory doesn't mean much fun for your Minecraft world if you can't actually do anything with Redstone gates. But, since this is a video game, Redstone gates are primarily used to create really fun and/or impressive things in your Minecraft world such as hidden doors, traps, cool lighting rigs and even super complex things like working computers and most of the mini-games you play on Minecraft servers.

In the end, the easiest way to explain Redstone gates in Minecraft terms is to say that they are what allow all of the really complex Redstone builds to work. The end result might be that a pirate ship battle mini-game kicks off in full force, but what you're not seeing when this happens is all of the Redstone gates and logic concepts that are built into the behind-the-scenes that allow the pirate ships to function and do things.

Using Redstone gates is not just important to mastering Redstone, it may be the most important part of the whole field outside of simply knowing how the various Redstone items work. It's not something that almost anyone can understand right off the bat, but if you take the time to try out all of these gates and think about how they work, and how to use them, we promise you that you'll come out the other side as a builder that's 100 times better at Redstone, if not more.

 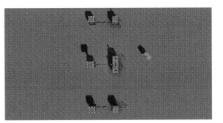

A Couple of Notes Before We Jump In

Before we start unleashing the mighty force of Redstone gate knowledge on your brains, a couple notes on what you're about to read:

The text for each gate explains how and why the gate works, and just gives a bit on how to build them. To actually build each gate yourself, simply copy what you see in the photos and diagrams. Make sure you do it exactly, or else the gates just won't work right. You'll know that you built it right if you get the same results in terms of turning the inputs ON and OFF as you see in the text below the title of each gate.

There are many, many ways to build each of these gates. What we've given you here is 1-3 basic versions of each of the gates that are easy to build and understand, but there are so, so many more ways to build each of them. This is because the rules that make the gates work can be used to construct them in various ways, from ways that are more complex to those that are quicker to those that take more inputs to those that travel in different directions (such as vertically, instead of horizontally). There are hundreds of variations on these builds available online, but for the sake of space, we've stuck to the most common versions for this book. We encourage you to play around with Redstone and see if you can come up with other ways to build these gates, or go online and copy a few layouts from the web to learn even more about them.

This is a very, very basic introduction to logic and electronic circuitry, but there is almost infinitely more information out there on both of these subjects. In fact, each of these would not only take up a whole book on its own, but many hundreds of books could, and have, been written on each. While this book and Minecraft itself are excellent introductions to the concepts behind logic and electronics (we'd say maybe even the best introductions yet), they are not meant to be the whole of knowledge on the subjects, and are really only scratching the surface. Again, if you're interested, seek out info online and even in libraries or schools if you want to know more.

Time to build some gates!

The Gates

INPUT/OUTPUT Gate

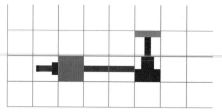

Diagram designed at mordritch.com

ON=ON
OFF=OFF

Short Translation: The signal that is input is the same as the signal that is output.

What it does: The INPUT/OUTPUT gate is really just a regular power source attached to a regular outgoing Redstone wire, but it is still technically a gate. Unlike our other, more complicated examples of logic gates, the signal that is put into the INPUT/OUTPUT circuit is the same as the signal that is output, making it quite simple.

Construction: A Redstone power component powers a block that then has Redstone transmission components carrying that signal away from the block.

Redstone Gates

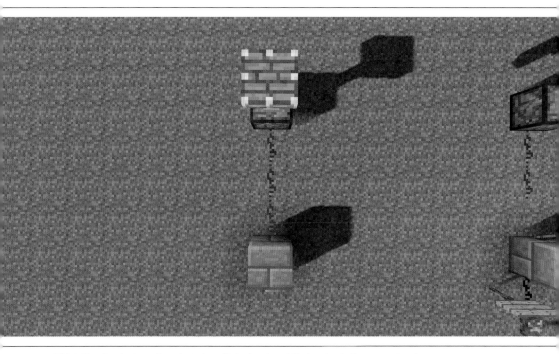

This is the simplest version of a gate, with just an input that outputs the same signal.

If you've learned how Redstone power components can send a power signal through Redstone Dust and other Redstone components when they are turned on, then you also understand the idea behind an INPUT/OUTPUT "gate," because this is pretty much how it works. We include the INPUT/OUTPUT gate (when it's not really any different from regular Redstone powering) because it gets us thinking in "circuit language," which is different from thinking of regular Redstone concepts.

In the case of the INPUT/OUTPUT gate, think of it as a gate that has an ON (or 1, to use binary terms like a computer does) input and an ON output (1), or an OFF input (or 0) and an OFF (0) output.

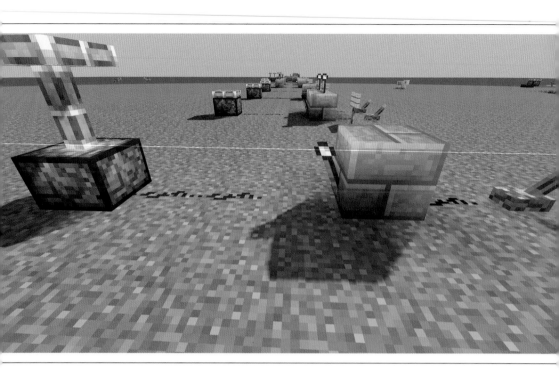

NOT Gate

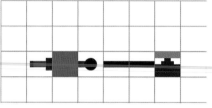

Diagram designed at mordritch.com

ON=OFF
OFF=ON

Short Translation: The signal that is input is the opposite of the signal that is output.

Also known as: Inverter gate

What it does: The NOT gate reverses whatever signal the input is giving and outputs that reversed signal. So, if the signal going in (input) is ON, the signal going out (output) will be OFF. If, on the other hand, the signal going in is OFF, then the signal going out will be ON.

Redstone Gates

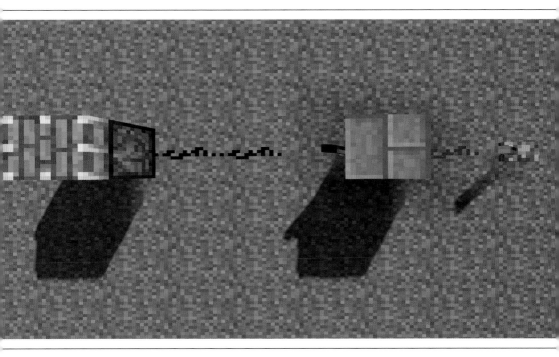

This is a gate that you will find yourself using time and time again, so remembering how it works will be very useful.

Construction: A Redstone power signal powers a block, and that block has a Redstone Torch attached to it, which is turned OFF when the Redstone power component is activated, or vice versa. Redstone transmission components carry that signal from the Torch to elsewhere.

NOT gates are the most important Redstone gate/circuit. They take an input signal and reverse it, meaning if the power going into the NOT gate is ON, then the output coming out of the NOT gate is OFF, and vice versa.

This ability to invert a Redstone signal is used often in builds, especially because other Redstone gates rely on the NOT gate to function. In fact, almost all other types of gates have a NOT gate built into them, or can have in some version.

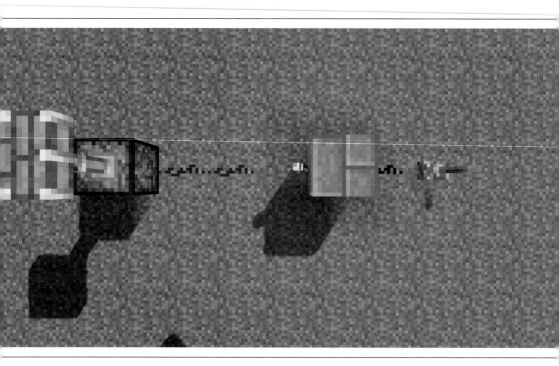

The NOT gate when the input is OFF

There is one very important feature that allows NOT gates to work; in fact, it's why they are used so often, and this feature has to do with Redstone Torches. The feature works thusly: when a Redstone power signal goes into an opaque block, it powers that block. A Redstone Torch attached to that powered block will be turned OFF. If the power signal(s) going into the powered block that caused the block to be powered (ON) is then turned OFF, the Redstone Torch turns ON. This is because it is no longer receiving an ON power signal, and so it has nothing acting on it. So, the Redstone Torch is then in its automatic ON state.

If you look at the images of almost all other gates in this chapter (excluding the INPUT/ OUTPUT gate and some of the simpler gates), you'll see that at some point the gate includes a NOT gate. You can see this when any single power signal goes into a block that has a Redstone Torch attached to it.

Redstone Gates

Another version of the NOT gate. There are many, many versions out there.

The end result concerning each gate's output status may vary, but if a signal is reversed at any point in a gate or a build, it uses a NOT gate. This ends up being thoroughly useful not only in circuits, but also on its own. For example, when you want a Redstone Torch to light up when a mob runs over a Pressure Plate. Typically, the Pressure Plate would send a signal to a Redstone Torch and turn it OFF, which seems counter-intuitive. When you build a NOT gate between the Pressure Plate signal and the mob-indicating Redstone Torch, however, you can invert the initial Redstone signal so that the Torch turns ON, and not OFF.

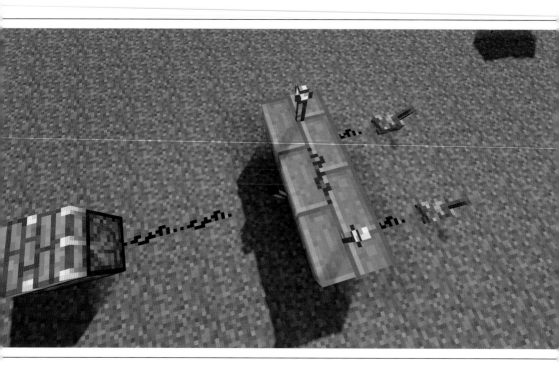

AND Gate

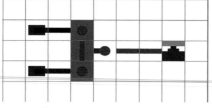

Diagram designed at mordritch.com

ON + ON = ON
ON + OFF = OFF
OFF + ON = OFF
OFF + OFF = OFF

Short Translation: The output signal is ON if both input signals are also ON, otherwise is OFF.

What it does: The AND gate requires that both inputs to it be ON for it to output an ON signal. Think of the output of an AND gate as a special light bulb that requires two switches to be flipped to ON for it to work: if no switches are ON, it won't work, nor will it work with just one switch ON. It must have both inputs ON to output an ON signal (or to light up, in terms of the bulb).

Redstone Gates

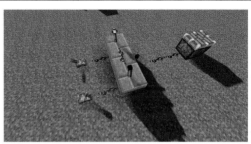

Note the state of the Levers and the Torches in each image, and which combined state causes the Piston to fire.

Construction: Two power signal inputs are each attached to their own NOT gate, and the outputs of those NOT gate are combined with Redstone transmission components and attached to a third NOT gate, which outputs a signal based on its two inputs.

Everything is in the name with the AND gate, and they're quite heavily used both in practical and in advanced logical builds. AND gates compactly combine the signals from two NOT gates to output a signal from a third NOT gate, meaning that the combination of the first two NOT gates outputting an OFF signal creates one ON signal outputting from the third NOT gate. If just one NOT gate in the initial two is outputting ON, or if both initial NOT gates are OFF, it causes the Torch for the third NOT gate to turn OFF, outputting an OFF signal.

Practically speaking, the AND gate can be used to create a situation where just knowing to flip one single Lever to send out an ON signal would not power a creation, forcing a player to know where both input Levers are and to flip them both ON. This is great for secret doors and other sly builds where you might want to hide one or both of the input power components (such as Levers).

Speaking in terms of logic, AND gates can be stacked with themselves and other gates to create complex patterns with varying results. For instance, try this example out: if both inputs to an AND gate are attached to the outputs of two other AND gates (in other words, there are two AND gates whose outputs feed into the two inputs of a third AND gate), you actually need both inputs for the initial two AND gates to be ON for the third AND gate to put out an ON signal. If even just one of the four total input signals across the two initial AND gates is OFF, then the third AND gate will output OFF as well.

OR Gate

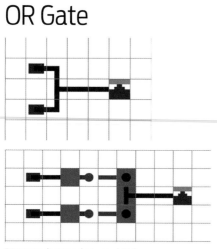

Diagram designed at mordritch.com

ON + ON = ON
ON + OFF = ON
OFF + ON = ON
OFF + OFF = OFF

Short Translation: The output signal is ON if any input signal is ON, including both. Otherwise OFF.

What it does: The OR gate is the opposite of an AND gate in that it always outputs an ON signal unless both inputs are OFF. In terms of real-life systems, think of this as a system that will turn on a light in a room if any of the light switches are turned ON, and will only turn off if all of the light switches are turned OFF.

Redstone Gates

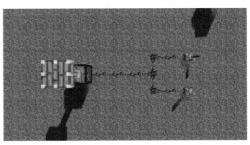

All three of these are OR gates, and the bottom left is built out of other gates. Can you tell which?

Construction: Like most Redstone circuits, OR gates can be built a variety of ways, including by just attaching multiple power components to a single opaque block with a Redstone signal leading out of it, or by leading a wire of Redstone Dust from two power components so that they combine into one wire. You can also build more complex versions featuring NOT gates.

OR gates are pretty simple to understand: if any ON power signal is going into the OR gate, the OR gate will output an ON signal. This is great for when you want a Redstone build to activate no matter which input is turned ON, and you can stack ON gates in a similar way to AND gates, but with the opposite result.

One thing to note with OR gates is that you might want to isolate the inputs from the gate itself so that you can use them to power other things as well without interfering with the gate. If you just combine Redstone Dust signals like in the above example, it will work, but it can cause problems if you want to use that same Dust signal for anything other than the OR gate (which is likely in complex builds like computers). This is not hugely important to know right now, but it's something to keep in mind.

NAND Gate

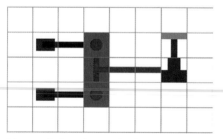

ON + ON = OFF
ON + OFF = ON
OFF + ON = ON
OFF + OFF = ON

Short Translation: The output signal is OFF if both inputs signal are ON. Otherwise ON.

Also known as: Neither-and gate

Diagram designed at mordritch.com

What it does: The NAND gate will output an ON signal if either of the input signals is turned ON or if both are turned OFF, so it will almost always put out an ON signal unless it is receiving a double ON signal, one from each of its two inputs. A NAND gate is an opposite to an AND gate in this way. All four gates are intimately related to each other, in fact, as you can see by comparing their INPUT + INPUT = OUTPUT charts.

Redstone Gates

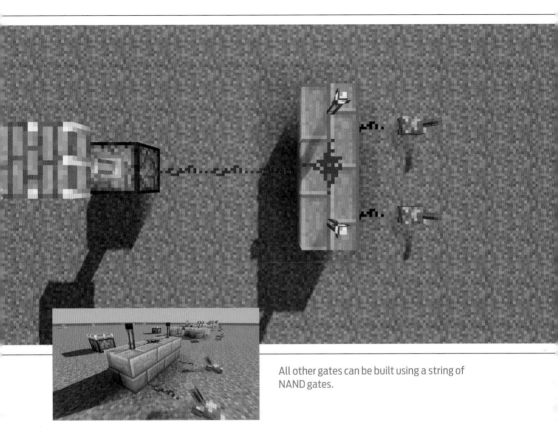

All other gates can be built using a string of NAND gates.

Construction: Easy NAND gates are exactly like the basic AND gate above, except that instead of having a third NOT gate taking the input of the initial two NOT gates, it just has Redstone Dust connecting the two NOT gates. Whereas in an AND gate the signal from either of the two initial NOT gates can cause the third to turn OFF or ON, in a NAND gate the signal from either of the initial NOT gates will cause the output to turn OFF or ON.

NAND gates are the logical extension of the AND gate, except in reverse. It's only when both inputs to a NAND gate are turned ON that it kills the output from the NAND gate. This can be used to deal with conditions when a Redstone build being activated would cause trouble if there was too much input (typically in complex logic circuitry).

For an analogy outside of the game, think of a high-security computer system that requires a signal from two administrators in order to be shut down. If just one administrator sends out their signal, the high-security system remains ON, as it needs both administrators' permission to shut off. This idea can be extended to Redstone circuits and mechanisms that almost always want an ON state.

NOR Gate

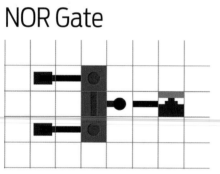

Diagram designed at mordritch.com

ON + ON = OFF
ON + OFF = OFF
OFF + ON = OFF
OFF + OFF = ON

Short Translation: The output signal is OFF if at least one, or both input signals are ON (either input can be ON). Output signal is ON if both input signals are OFF.

Also known as: Neither-or gate

What it does: The NOR gate will only output an ON signal if there is absolutely no ON signal going into it. This means that it is almost always OFF and is only set to be powered when everything going into it is shut down.

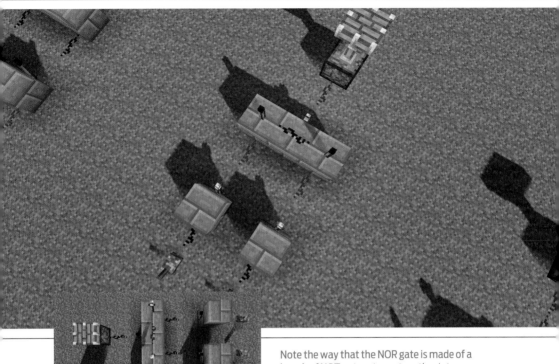

Note the way that the NOR gate is made of a bunch of NOT gates strung together into one output.

Construction: The NOR gate we use here is actually two NOT gates attached to the two inputs of a single AND gate. In fact, this is actually five NOT gates stuck together, creating a unique output. However, as mentioned before, there are other ways to build NOR gates.

NOR gates are kill-happy, which is a way to say that they will shut down if there is any ON signal going into them at all. They only output an ON signal if there is absolutely no ON signal going into them, making them very useful as kill-switches for your Redstone builds. Think of NOR gates as a build that is useful when you want to absolutely make sure the power is cut to a build unless everything attached to its input is OFF.

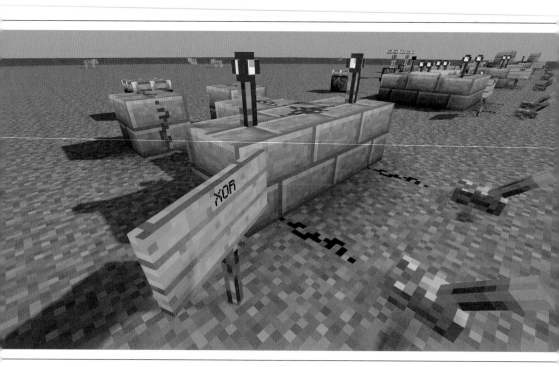

XOR Gate

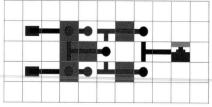

Diagram designed at mordritch.com

ON + ON = OFF
ON + OFF = ON
OFF + ON = ON
OFF + OFF = OFF

Short Translation: The output signal is ON if only one input signal is ON. Otherwise OFF.

Also known as: Exclusive-or gate

What it does: The XOR gate outputs an ON signal when its inputs are different from each other. Think of it like most normal real-life lighting systems that are controlled by two light switches: you can turn the lights on or off from either light switch by simply flipping one of the two switches. What you're actually doing is either causing that switch to be ON while the other is OFF, in

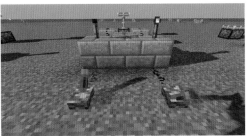

Two versions of the XOR gate, one of which requires Repeaters to function.

which case the lights are ON, or you're putting both switches in the same state (whether ON or OFF), in which case the lights are OFF.

Construction: Can be fairly complex. We've given two examples, one of which uses 7 NOT gates attached to each other, and the other of which uses the fact that Redstone Repeaters will only power things in front of them to make the design more compact with only 5 NOT gates. Essentially in both designs the various NOT gates check each other to make sure that only one single power signal is being input to the whole of the XOR gate at a time, or else the signals cancel each other out by the time they reach the final two NOT gates.

This is where we start getting into the somewhat more complex gates in terms of how much they take to build, how they work and what you'd actually use them for. To make it simple, XOR gates are a string of NOT gates that have the result of allowing one of two signals to control the XOR gate's output without having to travel to the other signal and turn it ON or OFF as well. This is useful for situations like the mentioned real-life lighting system that can be controlled from multiple switches.

Say, for instance, that you have a Redstone player trap in the land outside your base. You can hook up a XOR switch to Levers so that the trap can be activated when you look out the Door at the ground level of your base, or from up a Lever in a tower far above the ground. You can also then deactivate the trap from that same location without having to worry about running to the other Lever to deactivate it as well, as flipping just a single Lever for a second time will return the XOR gate to an OFF status.

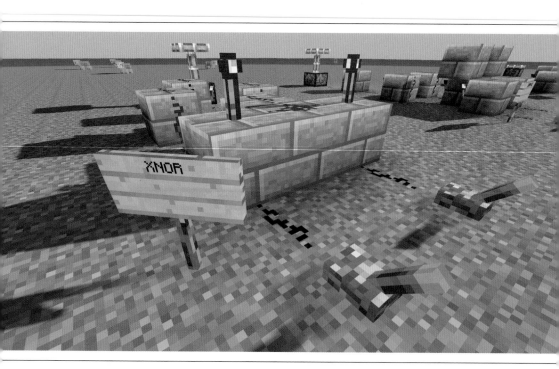

XNOR Gate

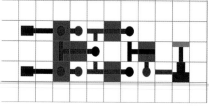

Diagram designed at mordritch.com

ON + ON = ON
ON + OFF = OFF
OFF + ON = OFF
OFF + OFF = ON

Short Translation: The output signal is ON if both input signals are the same, and is OFF if they are different.

Also known as: If and only if gate, equivalence gate

What it does: The XNOR gate is the opposite of an XOR gate in that it produces an ON signal when the two inputs are the same.

Redstone Gates

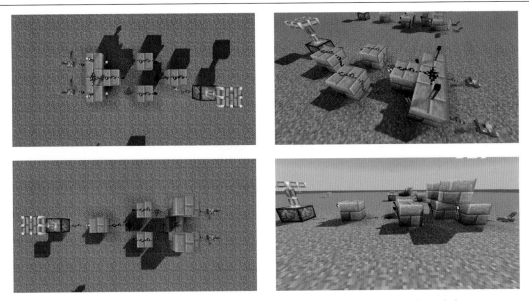

The XNOR latch is a lot more complicated than our other latches, but the rules are still simple for how it works. It's simply some of the other gates attached together!

Construction: The easiest way to think of it is to add a NOT gate to the end of a XOR gate, though it is slightly more complex than that. See images.

The XNOR gate is a weird one: it's like an AND gate, but instead of having to set both inputs to ON to make the circuit produce an ON signal, you just have to make sure that they're the same. This is both more complex and simpler than an AND gate: it's more complex because it takes more resources to build, and it's simpler because you don't have to worry about making sure that both inputs are set to ON, but only have to flip one of the inputs either to the opposite state to activate a system that is currently turned OFF.

Real-life systems where this could help include a system in which you'd always want there to be a person at each of the input controls, so that it had to be turned on with two people sharing the state of one of the inputs. However, this isn't necessary in the case of very simple systems hooked up to XNOR gates that activate immediately, but only in the case of those whose results are hard to determine immediately through visual means (so the knowledge of the actual state of the inputs is crucial to creating the desired outcome).

IMPLIES Gate

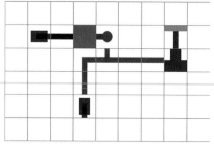

ON (A) + ON (B) = ON
ON (A) + OFF (B) = OFF
OFF (A) + ON (B) = ON
OFF (A) + OFF (B) = ON

Short Translation: The output signal is ON if input A and input B are both ON or both OFF, or if just B is ON. The output is OFF if A is on but not B.

Diagram designed at mordritch.com

Also known as: If-A-then gate, parent-child gate

Redstone Gates

A 1-high version of an IMPLIES gate, and one that is more compact horizontally but less compact vertically.

What it does: The IMPLIES gate is different from all other gates in that it has a primary or "parent" input and a secondary or "child" input. The output of an IMPLIES gate will always be ON unless the child input is ON and the parent input is OFF.

Construction: Consists of a NOT gate attached to the child input, which feeds into an INPUT/OUTPUT gate (i.e., just a straight line of Redstone Dust without any kind of inversion or other manipulation of the signal) that goes straight to the output.

The IMPLIES gate is another weird one, and it's unique among Redstone gates in that it is the only gate where the two inputs are not interchangeable. In the case of the IMPLIES gate, one input can essentially "block" the other input's signal, causing an OFF state even when the other input is ON. We call the "blocking" input the parent input, and the other input the child input.

These are very useful for when you want to have a signal usually propagate on through the IMPLIES gate and to the output, but in some cases would like to be able to shut off the signal without having to manipulate both inputs.

This, oh Crafter, is the biggest automated melon farm you have ever seen or are likely to ever see again by ToZaTop.

Automation
Making The Machine Do Work For You

One of the primary uses of Redstone is to take an activity that you typically have to spend a great deal of time on in Minecraft and to turn it into something that just happens at the flick of a few Levers. Well, that on top of spending a pretty good amount of time and resources setting up the system so it works right.

It's called automation, and it's one of the more practical uses for Redstone that there is. Where a lot of Redstone builds can be highly theoretical (Redstone gates, computers, etc.), fun/cool looking (drawbridges, doors, mini-games) or combat related (cannons, traps, mob detectors), automated builds are all about producing resources. Their goal is typically to take something like harvesting crops, cutting down trees, cooking meat or just about any other resource collection routine and to do the dirty work for you, leaving you with a lot of free time and a big pile of goodies.

Now, there are just about as many ways to do every kind of automated build as there are people who have attempted to build an automated system in the game, and many of these are quite complex indeed. While we unfortunately don't have the space in this little book to lay out the nitty gritty details of these monster machines, we can give you some ideas on what can be automated, and a little on how to start down the path of getting Redstone to do the hard work for you.

Farm Help

Sadly, without mods it's impossible to fully automate farming with just Redstone, as even Dispensers and Droppers won't plant a Seed into the ground. Villagers can be used to do this planting, but this is more of a breeding and herding method than anything that Redstone can help with much. What most certainly can be done with Redstone and farming, however is both to make plants grow faster and to harvest the fully grown materials when they're ready- both time consuming tasks that are nice to pass on to the machines.

Bone Meal Distribution: Dispensers that are stocked with Bone Meal and which are pointing at a plant that has growth stages (meaning trees and every plant that is or can be turned into food, including Mushrooms, which turn into Huge Mushrooms) will get the same result that a player using Bone Meal on that plant would. Which is to say, it makes them grow quite fast. This is a fairly expensive operation to set up, as you'll need a Dispenser pointing at each and every block that you'd like to get growin' a little faster, but if you rig up a whole farm this way, you'll never have to worry about waiting to get that sweet, sweet food again.

Auto-Harvesting: This term typically refers to two things: harvesting plants with Redstone-released (and then contained) Water, or harvesting with Pistons. Either way, it involves using Redstone to force something over the block in which a plant is growing, which automatically breaks it. If using Water (called a "Water scythe"), this is often done in a terraced format, where a farm is built in layers either on top of each other or in a staircase-like set-up (with each layer being no bigger than 8 blocks long, as that's as far as Water will flow without a drop in height). A Water source is usually blocked up with a Piston for this method, and is then released for a brief moment when a power component is triggered. Water is also great at carrying the harvested plants along with it as it flows, and smart farmers will build a place for that Water to flow, so the harvested materials can collect for pickup.

Piston harvesting works similarly, except a Piston must be set up adjacent to the block where each plant grows. When the Piston fires, it will break the plant and leave it as an item. Unlike Water scythes, Pistons don't collect all of the farm's plants in one spot, so these kind of automated farms usually have Hoppers to collect the plants, or the farmer will just run through and do it manually (aka the old school).

A cute, but deadly, automated cooker of Porkchops and Steaks by TotalVampireGirl.

Tree Farms

Like that of other plants, tree farm automation still requires that you plant Saplings by hand, and the automation part is also using a Dispenser to make the Sapling grow with Bone Meal, but there's another element to it with trees. While you can't get the tree to chop itself down, unfortunately, you can get Redstone working to make just about as many choppable tree logs as you like without you having to do much more than stand and smash down the Sapling-planting mouse button.

This is done, surprise surprise, by putting a row of Pistons right next to where the tree will be forced to grow by the Bone Meal. The tricky part is that these systems use block update detection methods (BUDs, see the Advanced Wiring chapter) to recognize that a tree has grown, which causes a block update. This then triggers the Redstone circuit that causes the Pistons to fire, and the Pistons shove the wooden part of the tree one block over (doesn't mess with the Leaves). This allows the player to just sit and continue planting Saplings while the Dispenser makes the trees grow automatically and the Pistons keep pushing them, creating a solid, long, tall line of Wood that can be chopped down all in a row.

Auto-Cookers

Automatic breeding is pretty tricky, but auto-cooking of meat is something that can definitely be done in vanilla Minecraft. There are quite a few methods to this, but essentially they all contain three things: a cooking area, a way to get food mobs into a cooking area and keep them there, and a way of putting flame to the animals to kill and cook 'em up. Fancy versions will also use Hoppers to collect these cooked delicious meats.

In terms of the Redstone, the typical method is to use Redstone in the "getting mobs into the cooking area" part (whether by having them fall through trapdoors, pushing them with Pistons or by some other method) and/or in the cooking part. One such method for cooking is to use Dispensers to drop Lava on mobs, but there needs to be some way set up for the Lava to only touch the mobs enough to set them on fire. If the Lava sticks around on the ground, it will just consume the cooked meat when it's dropped. Players have found various ways to get around this, such as using Lava in a contained space that has items such as Signs bordering its bottom layer, which Lava and Water will both just float above. This allows the player to drop the Lava with a Dispenser, light the animals, then suck the Lava back up quickly without the animals dying too fast and dropping their meats into the fiery, item-greedy liquid.

Other killing methods will also result in food, such as using Pistons to shove mobs into holes and past fire, drowning them in Water, or to use Flint & Steel, Fire Charges or Arrows in Dispensers and fire them at the mobs. Only fire-involved methods will cook it for you, however. Which is, of course, way cool.

Smelting and Brewing

We talked about this quite a bit in the entries for Hoppers in the Items chapter, but smelting and brewing can be fully automated in Minecraft using Hoppers attached to Furnaces and Brewing Stands, respectively.

All you have to do to get the process started is to hook up Hoppers to the top and side(s) of the Furnace or Brewing Stand, and then have the correct items go into the Hoppers. This will automatically fill the empty slots for smelting or brewing, causing the process to start. You'll also want a Hopper underneath these guys to catch the goodies, but note that this will not result in you getting any experience, and Hoppers can sometimes pull Potions from Brewing Stands before you've fully completed them.

The complex part is how you get the necessary items into the Hoppers. This can be done either with simply dropping them (not cool and automated, but works), or in much neater ways by putting Chests filled with the right items above the Hoppers. Even more cool, you can use Rail systems that use Minecarts with Chests that carry the needed items to the Furnaces or Brewing Stands. Some folks even get realllllly complex with this method and can customize the things brewed or smelted by putting just a few of the ingredients for each desired item into

Screenshot: Minecraft® ™ & © 2009–2013 Mojang/Notch.

the slots on the Hopper, causing it to only pick up more of those items in those slots, or by using special Minecart systems that specifically send carts loaded with only the wanted items to the Hoppers. Take it up yet another notch by adding an automated storing/sorting system to the end of the chain, which will sort/store the items that are brewed/smelted for you.

Sorting and Storage

Now this is where automation works quite well, and almost seamlessly. Using the rules of Hoppers and Minecarts and Chests (and Minecarts with Chests/Hoppers), players can set up very complex systems that collect, move, sort and re-distribute every item in the game that can be made into an entity (which is just about all of them except mobs).

Straight-up storage without sorting is quite easy: all you need to do is use Hoppers to move items into Chests for you, whether done in a stationary method or through a Rail system. Concerning the latter, you could, for instance, build a Rail system from the bottom of your mine back up to your base proper. You could then fill a Minecart with Chest up with your mining haul while at down at the bottom of your mine, and then send it back up using Powered Rails. If you've put a Hopper or so attached to a Chest under the Rail system at various points, the Hoppers would pull your items from the Chest, allowing you to send your items off to storage without even having to leave the mine.

In terms of sorting items, the primary way this works is as mentioned in the previous section: a Hopper will only pick up items if it has room for it in its inventory. This not only means having less than a full stack of items in each slot, but also that Hoppers that have an item in each one of their slots can only pick up more of those specific items. This is because each type of item must have its own slot in an inventory and won't be able to stack with other types of items. Using this feature, we can put items of a certain type (or a few types, up to 5) into each of a Hopper's slots, and then it will only pick up more of those items. If this Hopper is then attached to any other sort-of container, that container will only be filled with the same type of items that the Hopper contains.

Thus, if you set up a Rail system under which there was a Hopper that had only Redstone in it, another Hopper that had only Stone in it, and a third Hopper that had only 5 different food types in it, and each of these Hoppers was attached to its own Chest, you could then send a Minecart with Chest over the Rail carrying Redstone, Stone and food all mixed together, and as it went over the various Hoppers, they would sort these items into their individual Chests for you.

Auto-storage and sorting does use Redstone quite heavily, but it's more about knowing how to build good Rail systems and Hopper set-ups than it is building circuits (though this is not exclusively the case), and it can be a quite powerful tool for large projects.

Left: This sorter will sort a ton of types of items in no time. By DvirWi. Right: And this cooker will do the same, except with Cows, and killin'. By pg5.

Mob Farms

One of the more common uses for automated systems in Minecraft is mob farming. This is just what it sounds like, which is turning the killing of mobs (here we're using the term to mean non-food giving mobs) and the collecting of their items into an automated task. This keeps the player from having to go hunting, which is at once time-consuming and dangerous, and can also give quite mixed results. Mob farming, on the other hand, is safe, fast and always effective at procuring the player large quantities of materials.

Mob farms that involve Redstone typically do so in order to expedite the death of the mob, whether by using Pistons to position the mobs in desired places, using Dispensers, Pistons or other systems to kill the mobs, or for other reasons, such as temporarily releasing Water to wash all of the mob farm's drops to the player (similar to a Water scythe).

Storage and sorting systems can also be attached to mob farms, even in so much as to actually pick up the mobs themselves and move them from their spawning area to the "grinding" location, meaning where they're killed.

Note, it's totally possible to build mob farms without any Redstone at all, and it may often be more practical to do so. However, Redstone-using mob farms are usually pretty fun to both use and to build, and we think they're also pretty great exercises for novice Redstone engineers.

Redstone Challenge

See how many ways you can use Redstone and Redstone items to create a killing floor for a mob farm, then try hooking up a few different systems for collection and/or sorting. Do you prefer that the mob drops get swept up by Water, or can you make Hoppers do the work for you? Or maybe...both?!

5 Intermediate Builds

You've read about all the items, you've tested out a few builds, and you even know how to build a Redstone gate or two: it's time for some more difficult builds.

The coolest thing about Redstone, perhaps, is that the more difficult the builds get, the more fun and impressive they tend to be. In this chapter, we're going to really start getting some awesome stuff built with our favorite glowy, red material, starting with some sweet new doors for your home, and ending with the terrible might of a couple neat Redstone cannons.

At this point, we're going a bit beyond just making builds, and should be thinking about how they work and how to make them better. We'd suggest that you make each of these by the book (literally) once, and then play around with the ideas and see if you can't come up with more complex or, alternatively, simple ways to do them.

For now though, strap in, fire up your game, and get ready to impress your friends with these five super awesome Redstone builds.

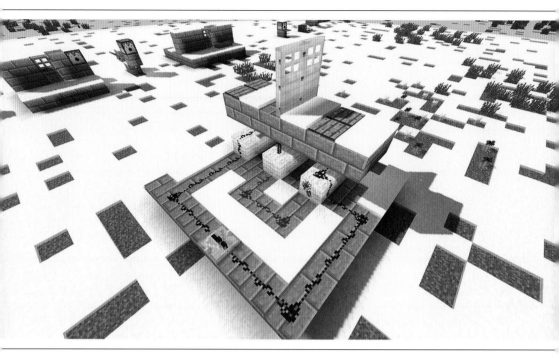

Automatic Double Doors

What it does: Automatically opens both Doors in a set of double Doors at the same time as the player runs across any of four Pressure Plates, two behind and two in front.

How it works: Just two little NOT gates, one hooked up underneath each Iron Door, that are then connected to two more NOT gates. The second pair of NOT gates is hooked up to four Pressure Plates, and it also causes the second set of gates to be OFF until it gets a signal from those Pressure Plates. Pretty easy!

You'll Need: 2 Iron Doors, 4 Pressure Plates, 4 Redstone Torches, 1 Redstone Repeater, 26 Redstone

It's kinda weird, but to get a set of double Doors in Minecraft to open and close at the exact same time is not as simple as just hooking them up to basic Redstone. While you can get them to act as one unit, one Door will usually fire open slightly behind the other. This is due to the amount of time it takes the Redstone signal to propagate from one Door to the next, and while it's not really a big deal, it's not the cleanest or coolest way to get your Doors to open.

Automatic double Doors that work well is a bit of a badge of honor among Redstone creators, and it's used by some as a mark of a person who actually does know a bit about the system. Our first intermediate Redstone build, then, is to get a double Door construct working that will fire both Doors at the same time when you run over Pressure Plates, and we'll use a few of the lessons we've learned about gates, specifically NOT gates, to get it working.

It's actually a pretty simple system to set up, though it takes a bit of space under your Doors. All it really is, is one pair of NOT gates under the Doors themselves that is hooked up to a second pair of NOT gates. That second pair keeps the first one OFF, and then the signals that the second gate sends are turned OFF themselves when the Pressure Plates the second NOT gates are attached to are activated. This allows the Torches in the first pair of NOT gates to go ON at the exact same time, opening both Doors simultaneously. **Nifty!**

1. Find a spot where you'd like to have your autodoors. This is a bit tricksy, as you're gonna need to dig out at least 3 blocks of space immediately below your Doors and Pressure Plates. For your first shot at this, as always, we highly recommend trying it in Creative Mode. Barring that, it's best to do this very, very early on when starting a base, as trying to add it in later can be a huge pain.

2. Place your Doors down.

3. Place your two pairs of Pressure Plates down in front of the Doors. Each pair should have 1 block of space between it and the block the Doors are on. Note: this is not 1 block of space including the block the Doors are on. If you don't leave space between the Pressure Plates and the blocks that the Doors open up into and are on the edge of, the build won't work.

4. Dig out space underneath the layer that the Doors and Pressure Plates are on. Leave the layer they're on, but the two layers immediately below should be totally clear in a decent-sized area. You can fill in some of this space later, but we suggest making it rather spacious to begin with (must be at least 7 blocks long in the direction that the Doors are facing, 8 the other way horizontally and 2 deep). This should be one block off-center of where the Doors are, as you see in the image.

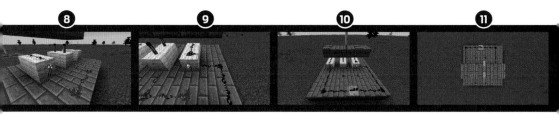

5. Place 2 blocks on the floor immediately below the blocks that the Doors are on, leaving a 1 block space of air between these new 2 blocks and the blocks the Doors are on. Do this for the Pressure Plates as well. See picture for reference.

6. Place 2 Redstone Torches on the blocks underneath the Doors (Doors will open for now). Place a Redstone Dust on each of the 4 blocks that are underneath the Pressure Plates.

7. Place a Redstone Torch on the sides of both outside ends (the side 1 block wide) of one of the sets of blocks under the Pressure Plates. Do not do this on both sets, just on one. See image.

8. Connect these Redstone Torches to the blocks underneath the Doors with Redstone Dust. Connect the left Torch on the blocks under the Pressure Plates to the left block under the Doors, and the right Torch to the right block, as you see in the image.

9. Place Redstone wire down coming off one Redstone Dust on the block pair that has Torches on its sides, and place this new wire on the side of the block pair that does not face the blocks under the Doors. What you've just created here, for reference, is two NOT gates under two of your Pressure Plates that lead into two NOT gates under your two Doors. See image.

10. Extend this Redstone wire according to the pattern you see in the image, so that you connect it to the wires on the block pair that has no Redstone Torches without creating a connecting between this new wire and the wires you placed in Step 8. That this strand of wire does not touch the other two is imperative to the build working. This wire is to carry power from the second set of Pressure Plates to the circuit you've built in the previous steps.

11. At some point in the wire you'll need a Redstone Repeater to keep the signal up, so place one down in the wire as you see in the image. Make sure to place this Repeater so that the signal carries to the blocks with the Torches, and away from the blocks without them.

12. Check your build with the images, and test out the Pressure Plates to see if it works. If you've wired it up correctly, stepping on any of the Plates will cause both Doors to open automatically.

13. Bury that build, making sure not to break any of the connections or to put opaque blocks in a place that would break them.

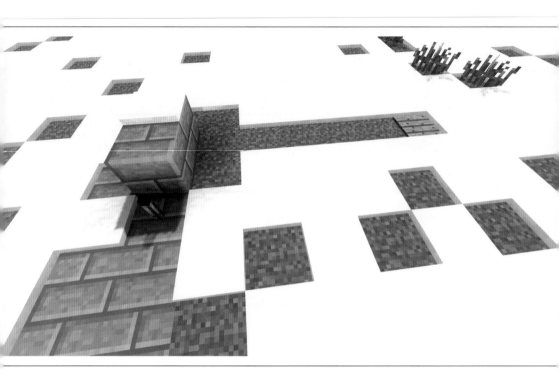

Mob Detection System (or- Day/Night Detector)

What it does: A Redstone Torch in your base turns on when mobs or players run across Pressure Plates in an area you'd like to keep tabs on.

How it works: One or more Pressure Plates is set up outside a base wherever you'd like, and Redstone Dust is run through an underground tunnel a layer below the Plates. This connects the Plates together, and the Dust then goes through the tunnels underground and back to your base or another area where you'd like the mob detection signal to go off. This Dust is hooked up to a NOT gate that leads to a Redstone Torch (a second one, not the one in the NOT gate), which is activated when anything triggers one of the Pressure Plates.

You'll Need: 1 Pressure Plate (any kind), 2 Redstone Torches, Redstone (a decent amount, will vary depending on your build), Daylight Sensor (optional)

One thing any veteran of Minecraftery knows well is that mobs and players can often sneak up on you when you're underground or in a base. It's hard enough to see all around your home even with windows, much less when you're deep underground or in other spots where there's no line of sight to the surrounding area. Usually there's not much you can do except listen (if close enough) and hope you can tell which direction mobs are coming from, but with this Redstone mob detection system, those days of wondering if a Creeper's outside will long be gone.

It's a fairly simple idea: Pressure Plates set up around the area where you want to be alerted to the presence of mobs and players will activate when something runs over them, causing a signal to go to a Redstone Torch in your base. When that Torch (or Torches, if you get fancy with it) lights up, you know that you've got intruders.

The only real tricks to this build are that you'll need to carve out a pretty decent amount of underground space to tunnel the Redstone from your Pressure Plates and into your base, and you'll also need to hook up a NOT gate before the final Redstone Torch so that it goes ON when a mob or player hits the Pressure Plate, and not OFF (you could just leave it without a NOT gate, but having a Torch go OFF when your system detects mobs is a little backwards in our minds).

This is easiest to set up with a small number of Pressure Plates and on the ground floor of your home, but you can add as many as you'd like and send the signal anywhere if you have the patience and resources to dig out all of the tunnels you'd need and wire it up. To send the signal for the detector up or down (say into a tower or cave), you'll need to either build wire staircases or ladders (see the Advanced Wiring chapter).

Another cool feature of the detection system is that it can even be hooked up to other Redstone mechanisms, such as the Pressure Plates that open a Door in your home, a Trapped Chest you want to keep tabs on or even just other Redstone circuits, so that you know when any of these is being used.

Note: Our instructions here are to build the most basic version of this contraption to show you how it works. In this case there will be just a single Pressure Plate and indicator Torch, and the distance between the Pressure Plate and the Torch will be very short. However, using the Redstone knowledge from the rest of this book, you can add more Plates, make the distances greater and even add multiple indicator Torches if you'd like. You can also hide the NOT gate in this build more cleanly than in some of the images here, as well as send the signal vertically if desired.

1. Dig a pit 2 blocks deep into the ground and 5 blocks long (this is just for this example build, it can be any length in your version).

2. Replace the ground-level Dirt block at one end of this pit. At the other end, replace the block at the floor of the pit. See image.

3. Place a Pressure Plate on top of the block that you replaced at ground level.

4. Place a line of Redstone wire across the bottom of the pit, including the space below the Pressure Plate and on top of the block at the other end of the pit.

5. Place a Redstone Torch on the ground outside of the pit at the end of the pit opposite from the Pressure Plate.

6. Put an opaque block in the space above this Redstone Torch, and then place a set of 4 blocks adjacent to the Torch and perpendicular to the pit in the pattern you see in the image.

7. Place Redstone Dust on top of the 2 blocks that are 1 block off the ground, as you see in the image.

8. Place a Redstone Torch on the side of the block that the Redstone Dust leads into. Make sure this is the block that you see in the shot, and not the one above the other Redstone Torch. This second Torch will go OFF immediately, because you have just created two NOT gates, and the first NOT gate (the one directly next to the pit) inverts the signal of the second NOT gate.

9. Test your contraption by stepping on the Pressure Plate. If set up right, the Torch you placed in Step 8 will light up (you'll have to place the Torch on the side of the block that's facing you to see it for now, as you're the one standing on the Plate, but you can move it back later if you want).

10. You can now think about expanding and refining this build. One obvious thing you need to do is to cover up the pit. In our example, you can just place blocks over all of the pit, though you'll have to place a block above the block at end of the pit that's next to the Torch, as you have Redstone Dust on the block below it.

There are many, many variations to this build- for instance, you could build the first NOT gate underground, and have the Torch for the second NOT gate (the indicator that goes on when mobs walk on the Plate) sit on the ground, as in the image. You can also add multiple strands of wire connected to multiple Pressure Plates that all go to the same Redstone Torch indicator, or you could give each Plate its own. Or, you could replace the Pressure Plate and the block it's on with a Daylight Sensor, creating a daylight indicator instead of a mob indicator.

Easy Combination Lock

What it does: A series of Levers acts as a combination lock for an Iron Door, forcing players to turn on the right set of Levers to open the Door.

How it works: An Iron Door sits on the block directly above the Redstone Torch in a NOT gate. If the wrong set of Levers (the wrong "combination") is activated, including none or all Levers, then a signal is going into this NOT gate, causing it to be in an OFF state. Only when the right combination of Levers is flipped will no power be entering the NOT gate, producing an ON signal and causing the Iron Door to open.

You'll Need: 5 Levers, 9 Repeaters, 4 Redstone Torches, 9 Redstone, 1 Iron Door

Keep friends and foes alike from getting into your home with this nice and simple lock build. This is a very cool little build that is quite impressive and which uses a good amount of Redstone theory without taking long to do at all. To explain how it works further, each Lever in the lock is on a block on the ground, and behind each of these blocks is a series of Redstone Repeaters and/or a NOT gate. The Levers that have just Repeaters behind them are the wrong Levers to pull to open the Door, while the ones with Repeaters and NOT gates are the Levers in the correct combination.

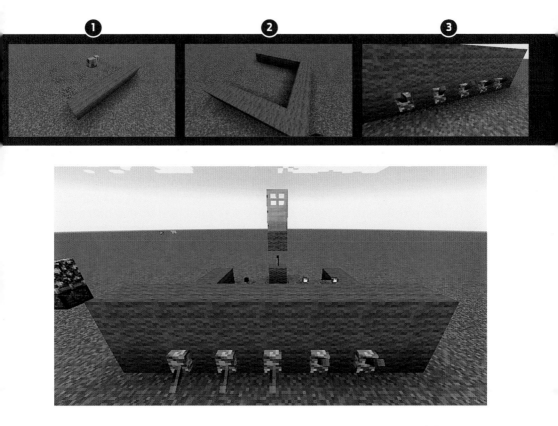

The way this works is that the Repeaters keep the lines of power from each Lever separate from each other (as Repeaters only give power in one direction) and a line of Redstone Dust perpendicularly connects the output to all of the Repeaters and the NOT gates. The signal of this Dust is funneled into just one line of Dust, which then goes into a final NOT gate. Above the Redstone Torch in this final NOT gate is the block on which the Iron Door sits.

When a Lever that is hooked up to just the Repeaters is flipped, it sends power all the way down to the final NOT gate, meaning any time any of the wrong Levers are flipped, the NOT gate is OFF and the Door stays closed. The other NOT gates in the build, the three that are behind the Levers in the combination, are automatically set to send an ON signal to the final NOT gate when their Levers are not activated, which in turn shuts the final NOT gate's output OFF. Each of the signals from the Lever-controlled NOT gates must be turned OFF by flipping its corresponding Lever in order for all NOT gates to stop sending out a signal.

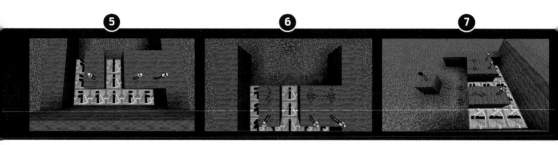

If any Lever-controlled NOT gate is still sending a signal to the final NOT gate below the Door, it will not open, and it will also not open if any wrong Lever is flipped, as this will also send a signal to the final NOT gate and turn it off. Only when all incorrect Levers are off and all correct Levers are on will there be no signal going to the final NOT gate, and the Door will open.

We've built this lock here using Wool blocks for ease of build, but the best idea for this construct is to use blocks that are quite difficult to break open, as you want to hide the Repeaters and NOT gates behind the Levers so that people can't see the combination. When done right (especially on servers where you can designate some blocks as unbreakable), it's a very effective deterrent to those who don't know the combination and are unwilling to sit and figure it out.

We also suggest, again, that you build this lock in Creative Mode or in a new base first, as opposed to adding it to an existing base, as it takes up a lot of space.

1. Build a line of blocks 7 long.

2. Place 5 more blocks coming off of each end of the line of 7, as in the picture. We also went ahead and added a second layer of blocks to the original 7 at this point, but this is not necessary to do until the end of the build.

3. Place Levers on the front side (opposite from the direction of the lines of 5 blocks) of the middle 5 blocks on the edge of your build that is 7 blocks long. See image.

4. Decide which 3 Levers you want to use for your combination. In our example, we picked Levers 2, 4 and 5 going left to right.

5. Go to the other side of the blocks from the Levers, and place down a row of Repeaters on the ground, all facing away from the Levers (so they're powered when the Levers are activated).

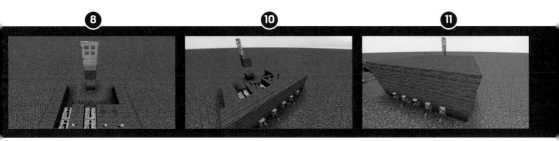

6. Create another two rows of Repeaters after this initial row of Repeaters, but only for the Levers that are not your chosen three for the combination. Instead of Repeaters for these three, you want to place 2 opaque blocks down, with a Torch at the end closest to the Levers on each set of 2 blocks. These are NOT gates, and they're what set your combination. See image.

7. Place Redstone Dust down on the second block in the pairs of 2 blocks that make up your combination columns, and then place Redstone across the ground behind the third row of Repeaters and the blocks you just put Dust on. See picture.

8. Place one Redstone Dust coming off the middle of the row of Redstone you placed in Step 7, and then place a block directly after that, and put a Redstone Torch on that block. This is another NOT gate.

9. Place a block directly above the Redstone Torch you just placed, and put your Iron Door on top of this block.

10. You can now go flip your Levers, and if it was built correctly, the Door will only open if the 3 Levers in the combination are ON, and all others are OFF.

11. You can then fill in the rest of the space around the door with blocks, hiding the contraption from sight! We suggest heavy-duty blocks like Obsidian, so that no one can break into your lock and find out the code, or destroy it.

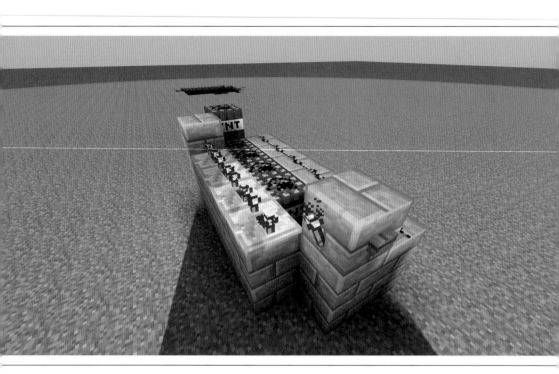

TNT Cannon #1- Easy Standard TNT Cannon (thanks to minegab for the design)

What it does: Fires a single shot of TNT a decent distance away from the cannon.

How it works: Uses the property of Water that says that activated TNT will float in Water and not blow up anything around it, but will blow up still and launch other activated TNT that is on a block around it. In this version, a single Redstone power component sends a signal down two paths- a first path that is that is straight Redstone, and a second path that starts with a NOT gate in an ON state and then goes through 4 Repeaters, and which is thus on a delay. The first signal instantly activates 4 TNT (called the "charge") that are laid in a channel with a Water source behind it, which then flows forward, catching the TNT and pushing it to the end of the cannon. The second signal turns off the NOT gate, goes through the 4 Repeaters and turns them off in turn, and this allows a second NOT gate at the end of the Repeater line (and which was therefore OFF before) to invert and give a power signal to a final block of TNT set above

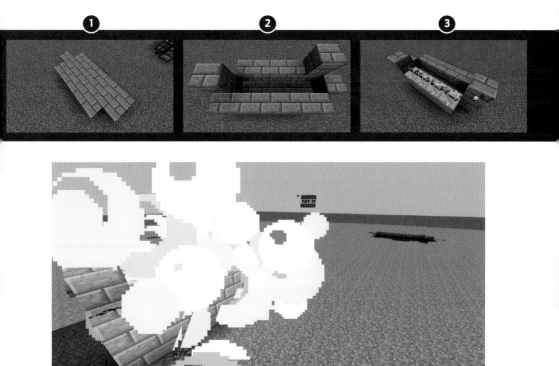

the others. This activates a few ticks after the rest, so when the 4 TNT explode, their force launches the final block of TNT out and forward, after which it shortly blows up itself.

You'll Need: 30 of any high resistance block (Obsidian is great, but at least use Stone), 5 TNT (more to reload), 4 Redstone Repeaters, 2 Redstone Torches, 6 Redstone, 1 Button, 1 Bucket of Water

TNT cannons are beast. Just about every Minecrafter loves these guys, and we'll bet that this cannon (or our second, even more beastly one) will be one of the very first Redstone builds you show off to your friends when you get it figured out.

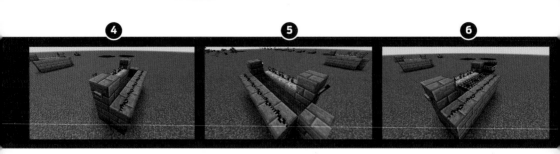

This particular model is one of the very most basic cannons, though it kicks things up a notch from the most simple TNT cannons by using just one split signal instead of two separate ones. Easier cannons don't use Repeaters, but instead use Redstone wire where the Repeaters in this build are, and they hook that up to its own Button. In that type of build, the Button that activates the "charge" (again, the TNT used to launch the final block of TNT, which is itself called the "shot") is pressed, the player waits for a few ticks, and then the second Button that activates the shot is pressed.

In our build, things are a bit more elegant. It does the job quite nicely, though the shot distance is not all that far, and the damage is fairly minimal. This cannon still has to be reloaded by hand to shoot again, but it makes for an excellent and quick lesson on splitting Redstone signals, using Repeaters and NOT gates, and manipulating TNT with Redstone. Plus, stuff blows up! Yay, stuff blowin' up!

A note: if for some reason your shot explodes before the charge, or if your charge goes off and it's not in Water, your TNT cannon will probably just blow itself up instead of your target. This is why we recommend you build the cannon out of sturdy stuff. If you build it right and it fires correctly, however, it doesn't matter much what you build it out of as long as it is opaque.

1. Build a pattern of blocks that copies what you see in the image here.

2. Build more blocks on top of this pattern of blocks the exact same way you see in this second image. This is the housing for your cannon.

3. On the end of the cannon with a block sticking out of the middle of the cannon, place a Redstone Torch on its left side. Add Repeaters facing away from this Torch to the left wall of the cannon, stopping when you hit the other of the two tall blocks on the cannon. See image.

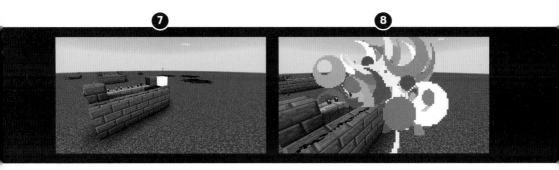

4. Go back to the tall block in the middle of the cannon, on which you put the Redstone Torch. On the back side of this block (opposite the length of the cannon), place a Button. Then run Redstone wire up the side of the cannon that's opposite to the Repeaters. Place this all the way down the side to the end.

5. Drop a Bucket of Water into the channel in your cannon on the side that has the block with the Button. Then add a final Redstone Torch to the far side of the tall block on the opposite side of the cannon (the one without the Button). Use the image for reference, and note that you need the Water to be flowing away from the Button.

6. Add one block of TNT on the single block sticking out of the far end of the cannon. It should be adjacent to the Redstone Torch at this end. Then place 4 blocks of TNT into the channel in the cannon, placing them starting from the end that holds the other TNT block and going back towards the Water source. Make sure not to place a block that covers the Water source, however, as this will likely result in the cannon exploding when you fire it.

7. Now, when you press the Button, the cannon will first ignite the blocks of TNT in the channel (the charge), dropping them into the Water, and it will then ignite the block at the end of the cannon (the shot). When the charge TNT blocks explode, they will launch the shot TNT block, if done correctly.

8. Reload, blow more junk up!

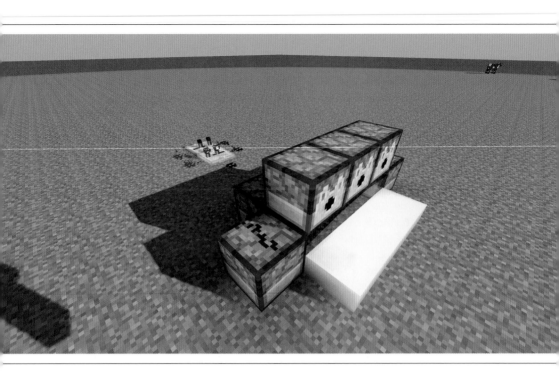

TNT Cannon #2- Rapid-Fire Scattershot Cannon

What it does: Fires a huge number of TNT shots 3 at a time a very large distance and covering an enormous area.

How it works: If you've read how the first cannon works, this one is much the same in basic principle, but kicks things up a notch or 500. Instead of hand-placing TNT blocks into a channel and activating them, this version uses Dispensers to repeatedly throw the "charge" TNT blocks into a Water channel set up directly above another series of Dispensers, which throw the "shot" TNT blocks above, slightly ahead and, in terms of time, slightly after the charge TNT blocks explode. This is done by building a fast pulser behind the cannon itself and then manually connecting it to Redstone already hooked up to the bottom row of Dispensers. You then wait a second or two before manually (and quickly!) adding another row of 3 Redstone that connects the pulser to the top row of Dispensers as well.

You'll Need: 8 Dispensers, a ton of TNT (whole heaps of it), 3 Slabs, 1 Lever, 2 Redstone Repeaters, about 17 Redstone Dust, 2 Buckets of Water, a few random blocks

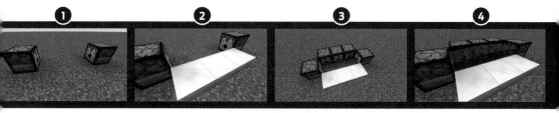

If you thought the first cannon was fun, wait til you get one of these bad boys firing. It's not exactly the prettiest build, as it's fired not by activating a power component, but instead by manually laying down extra Redstone and connecting it to a pulse circuit (aka a "pulser"), but in terms of glorious destruction and lookin' cool, it's pretty unbeatable.

It's also pretty simple to build, and it adds a bit more to the concepts we've been playing around with so far. It throws in the new idea of pulsers (more in the Advanced Wiring chapter) and adds Dispensers to the mix in a new way, this time using TNT. We also deal with the fact that we can't put the shot-firing Dispensers on top of the charge-firing Dispensers, as we need the shot to be activated at a different tick than the charge. This is also why we have to manually lay down the 3 Redstone Dust on top of the Dispensers slightly after the charge Dispensers are hooked up to the pulser. Speaking of, we also do a little bit of shift-click Redstone placement on our Dispensers here, another concept that is good to get familiar with.

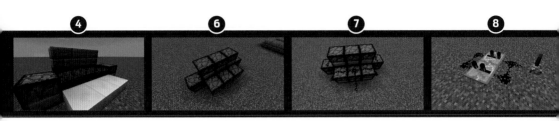

If done right (and it can easily go wrong the first few times), this cannon will spew out a wave of destruction and chaos that is almost unrivaled in Minecraft. So, don't point this thing at anything you like! It goes farther than you'd think, and it will outright decimate an area larger than a Village in mere seconds. In fact, we highly suggest pointing one of these at a Village at some point, just for the lulz.

1. Place 2 Dispensers facing each other with 3 blocks of space in between them.

2. Place a line of 3 Slabs one block forward and between these 2 Dispensers, as you see in the photo.

3. Place a line of 3 Dispensers facing the slabs, but 1 block back from and between the original 2 Dispensers, leaving a gap 1 block tall and 3 wide between the original 2 Dispensers, the 3 Dispensers in the back and the 3 Slabs in the front.

4. Drop 1 Water Bucket on the ground at one end of this gap, and then the second at the other end. You need to drop 2 total in order for this to work. Then put blocks of any kind on top of the 3 Dispensers that are facing toward the Slabs.

5. Place 3 more Dispensers on the side of the blocks you just placed, still facing the Slabs.

6. Destroy the 3 blocks you placed in Step 4, so that the back of the cannon looks like this image.

7. Place Redstone Dust on top of all of the Dispensers on the bottom layer of the cannon by holding the Shift key and clicking to place Redstone Dust like you normally would. Also add one Redstone Dust on the ground block at the two back corners of the cannon, and one on the ground leading away from the cannon. All of the Dust should connect, as you see in the shot.

8. Build a pulser a few blocks behind the cannon on the back side of it. To build a pulser, place 2 Redstone Repeaters and 4 Redstone Dust in the pattern you see in the image, and then send a signal into it. To send a signal into a pulser, you need to place a Lever adjacent to the Dust in the pulser, and then flip the Lever ON and OFF as fast as you can. If you did it right, the pulser will show a signal turning OFF and ON very quickly. If you did it wrong, it will show no signal or a steady signal, and you'll have to break the pulser's connection, re-connect it and try again with the Lever.

9. Fill all of the Dispensers with as much TNT as you'd like. Note that you need quite a bit in each for this to work, and only the TNT in the top 3 will be fired away from the cannon. The bottom layer of Dispensers is what fires the "charges," while the top is what fires the "shots."

10. To fire this crazy cannon (and it is quite crazy indeed), you need to perform a tricky maneuver. First, connect the Redstone Dust attached to the bottom layer of Dispensers to your pulser. Then very, very quickly jump on top of the bottom layer of Dispensers, wait about 1 second, then place a line of Redstone Dust on top of the top layer of Dispensers as well. You'll need to use the Shift key again to do this, and it will connect the top layer of Dispensers to the Redstone Dust on the bottom layer, in turn connecting the top layer to the pulser.

11. If done right, you'll almost immediately start seeing wave after awesome wave of TNT firing out in a wide spread from the cannon, going very far and outright wrecking all in its path. Again, we can't recommend enough that you try this on a village. It's really, really funny.

Redstone Challenge

Try to come up with ways to make this build's activation more elegant. Is there some other way you can come up with to get the bottom and then the top Dispensers to fire, instead of having to place Redstone manually? Would the top level have to be attached to its own pulser, or could it still use the same pulser as the bottom level, but still get the signal on a slight delay? And how could you go about sending a signal from the pulser to either set of Dispensers by using a power component to activate the whole contraption, instead of manually creating a Redstone Dust connection?

We've got a some ideas of our own, but try out a few things and see what you can come up with!

Advanced Wiring
Concepts and Terms

Before we jump into our final advanced build, let's talk a bit about some of the more advanced Redstone subjects. That's right kiddos; we're on to the crazy parts of Redstone now! Nice work making it this far.

In this chapter, we're going to give you an overview of some of the topics that Redstone engineers like yourself should start to tackle once they've got a firm foundation in the basics of Redstone. This is for when you'd like to kick things up a notch and learn more about the absolutely insane things people have been able to get Redstone to do when they really know their stuff.

We're just going to touch briefly on these advanced topics and give you a little info on each to get you familiar with them, as these topics could fill entire an entire book on their own and we just don't have the space. That being said, this brief overview will give you plenty of info to work with and should get you thinking about how to incorporate these advanced Redstone tactics into your own builds. If you're looking for more info, give each of these terms a search online, and you'll find more details by the truckload.

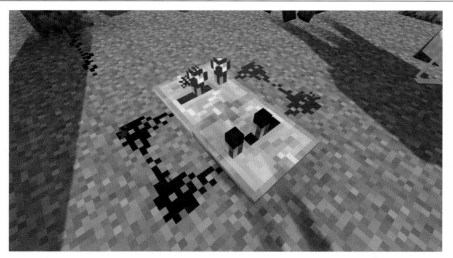

This is a basic pulser. You can't tell with the static picture, but this is blinking in a pattern.

Transmission Circuits

On top of the basic transmission items like Redstone Repeaters and Dust and the circuits we've discussed in previous chapters like our chapter on logic gates, there are a few other constructs that are commonly used to transmit a Redstone signal.

Bridge: Bridges are when one Redstone wire crosses over another without interacting with it. These can be created in a variety of ways, but the basic idea is simply that they are constructs that keep the two wires or circuits from interacting while still passing very close to each other.

Pulsers: As the name would suggest, pulsers or pulse circuits are parts of Redstone systems that send a signal that turns ON, then OFF, then ON again. These can be created in a large variety of ways, with the difference being the frequency of the pulse, the way the pulse is able to be turned ON and OFF (or not) and whether the pulse sends a signal in an ON>OFF>ON pattern, or in an OFF>ON>OFF pattern.

Detectors: Detectors are a variant of pulsers that create a specific type of pulse when certain situations are detected. "Edge detectors," for instance, create a pulse output at the moment of either detecting the beginning, or the end of another Redstone signal. "Pulse length detectors" output a signal pulse when detecting another pulse that is of a specific length, and "Comparator update detectors" pulse when they detect a Comparator that is updated by a change in a storage item's inventory. A fourth kind of detector is the "block update detector," or BUD, which is a very special and useful kind of detector that we'll talk about in its own section in just a few pages.

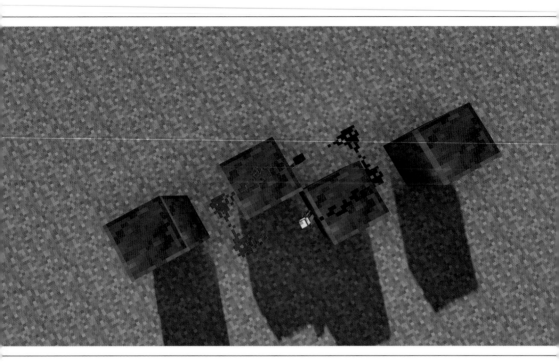

Memory Circuits

Where Redstone gates are constructs that take certain input signals into them and then output a new signal, meaning that their state is always a result of what is currently being input into them, memory circuits are able to take certain combinations of inputs and store a state based on which inputs have been recently put in. Essentially, memory circuits remember what inputs have been put into them, and they will keep remembering until other inputs occur. This is very similar to very (very, very) basic computer memory, as memory circuits typically stores 1 bit of information (either 0/OFF or 1/ON), though they can also store more. While there are a huge number of types of memory circuits that can be made, there are a few basic versions that people tend to use most often in Minecraft.

Latches: There are two basic types of memory circuits called latches- the RS latch and the JK latch. The RS latch is a circuit that takes two inputs, one which sets the RS latch to have an ON output, and the other which sets the latch to have an OFF output. One of the most well-known and widely used Minecraft circuits outside of gates is called an RS NOR latch, which, as you might have guessed, uses a NOR gate. JK latches are very similar to RS latches, except that when both inputs are ON at the same time, it will toggle the output from ON to OFF.

A basic T flip-flop. Knowing how to make these and what makes it work is something that really does separate a novice from a master Redstoner.

Flip-Flops: Like latches, there are two basic circuits known as "flip-flops"- the T flip-flop and the D flip-flop. A T flip-flop is another type of circuit that is used very often in builds, and it is also known as a "toggle," because inputting a pulse of power into a T flip-flop will cause it to toggle between an output state of ON and OFF. This means that when a pulse of ON power goes into a T flip-flop that is already outputting an ON signal, the T flip-flop will start outputting an OFF signal and will keep doing so until another pulse of power goes through it. D flip-flops, on the other hand, have two inputs: a clock (or C) that pulses power and a "data" input (or D) that holds a current state. When the C input pulses through a D flip-flop, it causes the output of the D flip-flop to be equal to whatever state that the D input is in while between pulses.

Counters: Counters are memory circuits that can store not just two states, but many states.

Using Torch towers is essential to powering most builds with multiple vertical layers.

Ladders, Torch Towers and Staircases

Redstone Dust is great for transmitting a Redstone signal horizontally, but when you need the signal to move vertically up or downwards, things get a bit tricky. Redstone Dust will typically only move a signal up in a staggered "staircase"-esque build, but creative players have managed to come up with a couple of other methods for vertically moving a signal, called Torch towers and ladders, respectively.

Staircase: The most basic method for moving a signal up or down, staircases look like their namesake, as they involve a block being one block above or below another and one block to the side. Redstone Dust can be placed on top of both blocks, connecting them, and a power signal can be sent through them.

Torch Tower: Torch Towers use the property of Redstone Torches that says that they will power an opaque block placed above them. By placing a block on top of a Redstone Torch, and then another Redstone Torch on top of that, and then repeating this a third time on top of this second Torch, we are able to move a Redstone signal straight upwards. This is actually creating multiple NOT gates stacked on top of each other, and is a very efficient way to transmit a signal vertically, though it does not work downwards.

Ladder: Ladders involve placing transparent blocks like Glowstone or Slabs in a vertical "checkerboard" pattern, placing Redstone Dust on each block as the ladder goes up. A signal can be hooked up to the bottom of a ladder, and because the blocks are transparent, it will propagate up the rest of the ladder. Also only works vertically.

Block Update Detectors

We talked about detectors a few pages ago, but to refresh, they are pulsers that create a signal pulse only when they detect certain conditions. Of the various detectors, block update detectors or BUDs are probably the most common and useful. These take advantage of a "bug" in Minecraft that causes Redstone circuits or mechanisms not to recognize that they should be receiving a signal until the game sends a "block update" to the area. Block updates are basically the game checking the state of each block and seeing if it should change, and they are triggered by actions or events in the game, including placing blocks nearby, Grass growing, a natural block of Redstone being punched or stepped on, and many other ways.

Though there are many types of BUDs, in all BUDs there is one block that is the "sensor" block, which is the block that does not realize it should be receiving an update. Players then force an update by causing one of the previously mentioned or other events to occur, the sensor block gets an update, and the circuit it is attached to receives a short pulse of power. The circuit then goes back to "sleep," and the power goes off.

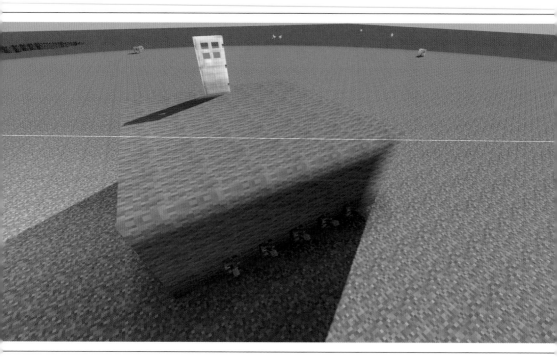

This build is said to be "hipster" because you can't see any of the wiring. In fact, this build actually is quite hipster, because even when functioning no wiring is exposed.

Redstone Building Terms

As practitioners of very complex subject, Redstone engineers have come up with many special terms to describe what they are creating. You've already heard many of them, but here are a few more terms to use that will help you to communicate info about your builds, not to mention impress your friends and other engineers.

1-High (Flat)/1-Wide- Refer to the shape and dimensions of a build. 1-high or flat builds are only 1 block tall, while 1-wide are only 1 block across in one direction.

Analog/Binary/Unary: Refer to the transmission of power through certain circuits where the state of the power and the type of circuit are used to represent numbers. "Analog" transmission means that the power level of the input of the transmission is the same as the output, and it can have 16 states (0-15 power). "Binary" transmission refers to transmission where multiple lines of transmitted power each have their own state, and where each state makes up one digit in a single binary number (binary numbers look like this- 1101100, 001, 0100 etc.). "Unary" refers to multiple lines of transmission where the number represented is selected by which of the lines of transmission is powered. So, if the 9th line of transmission is powered, the number represented is 9.

Cannon names: This is maybe the most complex subject in this chapter, oddly enough, and we don't have space to fully explain the complexities of naming cannons, but suffice it to say that there is a very specific system that players have created to name cannons which quickly tells other players information about that cannon. The formula for naming cannons is, to give the simple explanation, as follows:

[DV].[EV].[TA].[MR] [Cannon nickname]

Each value is a number, except the last.

DV= damage value (accuracy, power and speed combined)

EV= ergonomic value, meaning difficulty of build (average of construction, Redstone and TNT values)

TA= amount of TNT used

MR= maximum block range can fire

Cannon nickname= what the player calls the cannon

To learn more about this, check out the extensive article on the Minecraft wiki.

Flush: Flush means that the build doesn't extend beyond a flat floor, wall or ceiling and which provides power to the other side of the floor, wall or ceiling.

Hipster: Doesn't mean what you think, but instead means that you don't see any Redstone components before or after a Redstone construct performs its operation. A build is still "hipster" if you can see them during operation.

Instant: The output of a build activates right away after the input activates, with 0 ticks of delay.

Seamless: Seamless means that the build is totally hidden behind a flat floor, ceiling or wall when not activated, but which when activated interacts with the other side of the wall.

Silent: As you'd expect, these are builds that don't make noise. So, Piston builds usually aren't silent.

Stackable/Tileable: Terms that are opposites of each other, where stackable means that you can place multiple exact copies of a build directly next to each other, and the builds can all be controlled together as one, and tileable means that copies of the build can be placed directly next to each other and still controlled separately.

Final Lesson:
An Advanced Build

Now, it's time to put all of the knowledge you've (hopefully!) picked up from the rest of this book to work in a build that's more than a little complicated, and also more than a little awesome.

You know about Redstone gates, you've had a little bit of info on some advanced wiring concepts, and you've whetted your appetite for builds with a few beginner and intermediate options. But this, girls and boys, is the big one: the 3x3 Piston door.

Of course, the truth is that this build would actually be considered quite simple by many Redstone masters, but that's the beauty of Redstone: like all truly rich subjects of learning, each time you get to a point where you feel like you've understood something about Redstone, you realize that there's just so much more out there still to learn.

So, we aren't saying this is advanced by, say, Sethbling or pg5's standards (both could probably build this one handed and asleep), but for those who have just recently begun their journey toward Redstone engineering dominance, it most certainly earns the term

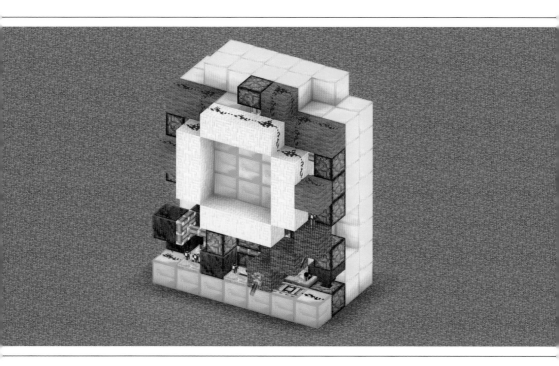

advanced. Firstly because this build exemplifies many of the most important qualities about Redstoning, including elegance, efficiency, circuits working separately and together, gates and more. And secondly, because when you build this Piston door, you can truly say you've done something awesome with Redstone.

Think of this as at once your final Redstone exam, and your final lesson. It's fairly simple to follow the instructions to build this guy, but the important part here is to think about why each part does what it does. We'll give you a little bit of the info, but we'd like to encourage you to do some of the discovery on your own, as nothing will solidify a lesson better than that eureka moment when you realize through your own thought processes what it is that makes a complex Redstone build truly tick.

All the info you need to understand this build is in the pages of this book, and there's ever more out there online and in the heads of the Redstone engineers building on Minecraft servers across the world. Build it, think about it, and don't be afraid to go back through these pages or to seek out an expert to get more explanation.

Once you truly understand what's going on in this build, well, we'll just say this:

Welcome to the Redstone engineering corps, miner.

Mumbo Jumbo's Tiny 3x3 Piston Door

What it does: Uses just one Lever to open and close a door made out of a 3x3 section of blocks that, when open, hide away into the structure of the build

How it Works: Essentially, it's a series of Sticky Pistons that extend and retract blocks from the side and the top of the door frame so that all blocks in the door are removed (to open) and then replaced when closed. It does this using three circuits, all controlled by one Lever. The power signal from the Lever goes to each circuit in turn. Different parts of the build is receiving power at different speeds due to the Repeaters in the build and because of various broken and unbroken circuits, which all causes the various Pistons in the build to fire at different times, pushing and pulling the blocks involved in the door at just the right time.

It's a rather elegant and easy(ish) to build contraption, yet is also fairly advanced in its composition, involving NOT gates, a mini Torch ladder, delayed signals, breaking and creating circuits, a monostable circuit involving a Comparator, a Hopper and a Dropper (more on that in the instructions) and a double extender Piston array.

Final Lesson: An Advanced Build

You'll Need: 12 Sticky Pistons, 1 Lever, 1 Comparator, 1 Dropper, 1 Hopper, 1 Detector Rail, 3 Repeaters, 18 Redstone, 3 Redstone Torches, many opaque blocks

The 3x3 Piston door is a bit of a legendary step in the process of becoming a master Redstone engineer. This is because it doesn't just involve solving a simple problem (i.e. "I need a door here"); it also contains a problem within itself. This is that a 3x3 door made of blocks has one block in the center that must be pushed and pulled along with the rest of the build to be truly well-done, but if we were just to build this door using Pistons surrounding a 3x3 space, no Piston would normally be able to reach that middle block. The other blocks in the door and the other Pistons would be in the way, meaning it would be left floating alone, looking terrible.

This means that we have to figure out a way to manipulate that block with Pistons as well as the others. This, oh miners, is the kind of problem that Redstone engineers love to solve. Being able to successfully create a build that solves problems like this is what separates a Redstone dabbler from a true member of the Redstone engineering corps, and it's a heck of a lot of fun along the way.

So how are we going to solve this problem? Well, as we said, we aren't going to give you the answers to how every single detail of how this build works, as we think it's important to leave some things for you to discover on your own, but the gist of it is this: we are going to set up some normal(ish) Sticky Piston arrays for the rest of the blocks around the middle block and the block below it, and we're going to build a special Piston design to take care of extending and retracting those two pesky middle blocks.

The basic idea of the build is that we're going to use a double Piston extender (aka a DPE) that will push first the middle, and then the bottom middle block up into the door one at a time. When it retracts, it will pull the bottom middle one out first, and then go back and grab the top middle one.

A third Piston will feed the second block (the bottom middle one) to the DPE after the DPE has pushed the first middle block in (when closing the door), and that same third Piston is used to pull the bottom middle block off the DPE after the DPE has snatched the block when the door is opening. This third Piston helping out allows the DPE to be clear to grab the middle block. It also, however, means that the DPE has to fire twice: first it fires so that just the top Piston in the DPE activates, grabs the bottom middle block, then retracts, and then the third Piston grabs the block from the retracted top Piston in the DPE and moves it out of the way. Second, the DPE fires again, and this time the bottom Piston in the DPE fires first, pushing the top Piston up, and then that top Piston fires too, grabbing the middle block. The top Piston in the DPE then retracts, and then the bottom one retracts too. This works in the opposite way when closing the door.

We know, it's a bit confusing, but once you see it in action it will make a lot more sense.

To get this to even happen, however, we have to build an array of circuits at the bottom of the door construct that cause power to reach the three Pistons involved in the pulling and pushing of the two middle blocks at specific times, and that power signal also has to be activated, be cut off, and be activated again multiple times with just one flick of a Lever, and it has to go to different pistons in the DPE trio at different times. To get this effect, we have to create some somewhat complicated circuits, including one on the left side of the build that uses a power signal that is delayed through Repeaters, which causes it to fire a Piston that pushes a block, which cuts itself off and then reactivates itself. We also have to build a circuit on the right side of the build that uses what is called a monostable circuit.

The rest of the Pistons in the build also have to fire in order to extend and retract the rest of the blocks that make up the door, and all of this has to be wired together to be activated by flipping just one single Lever. This means the build must carry a power signal vertically as well as downwards at points, and since the point of all of this is do the build in a very small area that can fit into most bases (7x2 blocks horizontally and 9 vertically), we have to be very, very efficient with how we get that current to travel up and down to the other Pistons.

Now you can see why this build is your final lesson in this book: it's not too hard to build when you have the instructions, but understanding it is something else entirely.

Redstone Challenge

While you're building this, don't just try to understand how it works, also try to think about how someone came up with this idea. There are many, many 3x3 Piston door designs out there, but this is one of the best and most famous because it is so incredibly efficient and compact. See if you can come up with another way to do it without worrying about how big it is. Then, see if you can take your version of the build and make it more compact. We guarantee you that if you weren't already amazed at the elegance and cheap item cost of this build before, you will be after you try your own.

Final Lesson: An Advanced Build

1. Build or mark off a 7x2 block area of horizontal space which will be the bottom of the build. We're going to be referring to the "front" and "back" of the build as well as the two sides, so pick one of the long sides and start thinking of it as the front of the build now. The portal for the door itself will have its bottom block at 5 blocks off the ground, so if you're building this in a base, make sure to keep that in mind. As always, we can't suggest enough that you try this out in Creative Mode before trying to fit it into a base.

2. Place a Sticky Piston facing up on the back middle block of the 7x2 area, and then another Sticky Piston facing up on top of that first Sticky Piston.

3. Place two more Sticky Pistons to the right of the first two Pistons as you see in the image here, still on the back row, but one should be in the right corner one block off the bottom of the build, and the other should be one block to the left and one block up from this first Piston. Make sure these two new Pistons are facing in toward the middle of the build.

4. Build an L shape out of opaque blocks on the right side, front row of the 7x2 area, leaving one empty block on the far right, as seen in the image. Put a dot of Redstone Dust on the leftmost block in the L, and put a Redstone Torch on the right side of the top block of the L. This is a NOT gate. Note that in our build we're using different colored blocks for each one of the three main parts of the circuits that make up this build, and we suggest doing the same so that you can keep better track of what's happening.

5. Go to the back side of the build and place a block immediately above the last Redstone Torch you placed, and place another Redstone Torch on this new block, but facing the back of the build. This is another NOT gate and is a small Redstone ladder.

6. Place a block in front of the head of the Piston that extended when you set the first Redstone Torch down (the only extended Piston, which is the one facing toward the middle on the bottom on the back of the build).

7. Move back to the front right side of the build, and remove the block at the bottom right corner of the L of opaque blocks. Replace that block with a Detector Rail. Set the Rail to face the way it is in the image, which is going left to right (you may have to put a second one down temporarily to do so). Put a line of Redstone Dust on the block to the right of the Detector Rail, as in the image. The Detector Rail doesn't actually function in the build except to make sure that the Redstone Dust faces it, and not any other part of the build (which is crucial).

8. Remove the back right corner block of the 7x2 base of your build and replace it with a Dropper facing up. Put one item of any kind in this Dropper.

9. Shift click and place a Hopper so that it is right above the Dropper and attached to it.

10. Place a Comparator on the empty block to the right of the Hopper (when facing the build from the back) so that it is facing away from the Hopper and toward the Piston two blocks to the right. Then put a block between the Comparator and that Piston. What we've built here with the Hopper and the Dropper and the Comparator is what is called a "falling edge monostable circuit." A "monostable circuit" is a circuit whose output will remain in the same state (ON or OFF) until a power signal is input into it again, and "falling edge" is a term that refers to a power signal being output only at the moment that an input power signal is turned OFF. This is a rather complex topic, but the gist of what happens is that when we flip the Lever that controls the build to ON, it causes the Comparator to read the inventory of

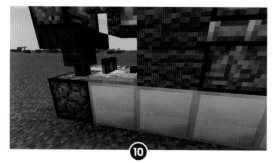

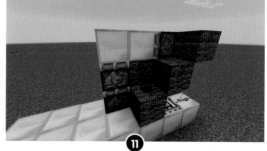

Final Lesson: An Advanced Build

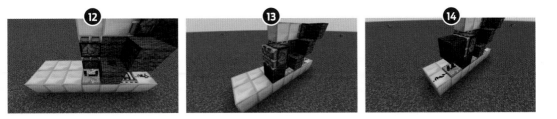

the Hopper, which is just pushing the single item back into the Dropper, and this Comparator pulses a single signal with a power level of 1. This happens at the end of the power pulse going through the build. This is important for our DPE because we need the top piston in the DPE to pulse (quickly activate and then deactivate) when we are trying to retract the middle blocks. This is the most complex part of this build in terms of theory, and there is a lot more info on these kinds of circuits online.

11. Return to the front of the build and place two opaque blocks, one on top of the DPE and one on the block to the right of this block you just placed. These blocks are what will make up the middle two blocks of your door, aka the blocks that cause all the trouble with 3x3 doors.

12. Place a Repeater facing left and set to 4 ticks in front of the bottom Piston of the DPE.

13. Place a block to the left of this Repeater (we are using a different color now because this is a separate part of the circuit), and place a Sticky Piston on top of this block facing left.

14. Place a block in front of the head of this Piston, and place a Repeater under this new block. The Repeater should also face left and should be set to 2 ticks. Place one Redstone on the block in front of this Repeater. This is the last block on the far left front edge of the build.

15. Place a block on the far left back corner of the build, and then place a block that is one block up and one block to the right of this new block (see image). Place Redstone on both of these blocks (it will connect to the Redstone you just placed in the last step).

16. Go to the back of the build and put a Repeater set to 4 ticks facing left (so it faces toward the direction of the Pistons in the middle of the build) under the block you just

Screenshot: Minecraft® ™ & © 2009–2013 Mojang/Notch.

placed last (the one that is one above the base of the build). Place a block directly to the left of this Repeater, and place Redstone Dust on top of this last block.

17. Place a block directly above the Redstone you just placed in Step 16 (see image, block should go 3 blocks from the base of the build). This block is important, as it cuts off the signal from the Redstone beneath it to areas of the build that should not receive it. You can now go back to the front of the build and place a Lever on the block to the right of the Redstone Repeater in the middle of the build and flip it to see the DPE in action. If set up right, it will push two blocks up into the middle of the build when flipped ON, and will retract them when flipped OFF. This is the hardest part of the build, so pat yourself on your back, because it's done!

18. Facing the front of the build, copy the row of 3 blocks and 3 Sticky Pistons seen in the image on the right side of the build. The Pistons should face inward to the blocks you are placing. Then add the top row of 3 blocks, with one Sticky Piston facing down directly into the top middle block. All blocks that you're placing that have a Piston facing into them are part of your door proper.

19. Complete the "circle" of the door by adding 3 more blocks and 3 more inward facing Sticky Pistons on the left side of the build, as seen in the image.

20. Move to the highest block in the front row on the right side of your build (in the image for Step 19 it is the magenta block on the far right of the image, and it also has a Redstone Torch on it facing to the back of the build). Put a Redstone Torch on the very top of this block (it now has two Torches, one on the back and one on the top). Place a block

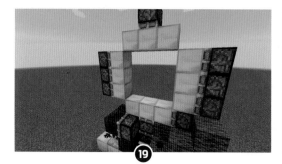

directly above this new Torch (we used a new color block for a new part of the circuit), and put Redstone Dust on top of this block. Don't worry about the Piston that fires here, it's supposed to.

21. Place another block one up and one to the left of the block you just placed, then another block that's one up and one to the back of the build from that new block, and then a third one that is one block to the right of that block as well (see image). Place Redstone Dust on all of these blocks.

22. Place a block to the right of the Piston that is on the top of the build and facing down, and put Redstone on this block (it will connect with what you have just placed).

23. Place 3 blocks, one in front of each of the 3 blocks that make up the top part of the door (the Piston is facing down into the middle block of these 3 top door blocks). Then place one block a block down and to the left of these 3. For the 4 blocks you are placing, you want to use a type of block that you like the look of, because this will be the frame around your door from this side. Place Redstone on all 4 door frame blocks you just placed.

24. Place 2 blocks on the back row of the build as you see in the image (one block up and back from the last block you placed, the one that was one block below the other door frame blocks). These 2 new blocks will be on the same level as the top of the door frame. Place Redstone on both of these blocks (it will connect to the single door frame block below these 2 new blocks).

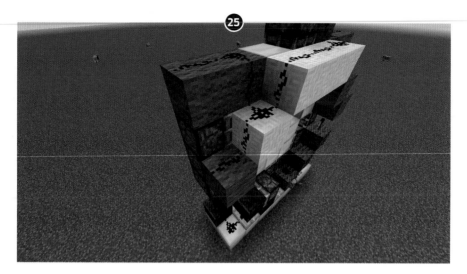

25. Place one block on the far left front edge of the build and 2 blocks down from the blocks you just placed (see image). Place Redstone on this block. It should connect to the single door frame block that is slightly below the other 3 door frame blocks. Your door is now fully powered!

26. Complete your frame with blocks of the same type, as seen in the image. You'll have to replace the top block on the right side of the frame with a frame block (instead of a circuit-colored block), and you'll need to replace the Redstone Dust on this block when you do so.

27. Go back down to your Lever, and flip it! If you did everything right, the Pistons will fire and the door will open and close as you flip the Lever. Make sure not to flip it too fast, however, as it takes a second to completely open and shut.

28. Congratulate yourself for being a Redstone genius-in-training!

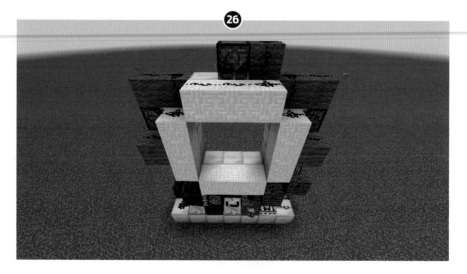

General Tips For
Wiring Up Your Build

Trying is the only way to make great Redstone, and it's the only way to get better.

Plans are great, but there will almost always be a problem. This isn't a bad thing; it's just how it goes with complex systems.

Learn the gates. Learn the gates. Learn the darn gates. You will not regret it.

Also learn the items. Learn all of the items, as leaving out even one will really limit your ability to create things as well as you possibly could. Learn good habits early, and they'll reward you forever.

Your build can almost always be more efficient or more compact.

But there's no "right" or "wrong" in Redstone. Just builds that work and builds that don't.

Think of Redstone as puzzle or problem solving. This makes it much easier to deal with. What is the goal, and what is the problem in the way of achieving that goal?

Compartmentalize your builds. By this we mean think in terms of small sections at a time. Don't try and do too much at once, or your project will become a mess. Solve one small part of the problem completely, then move on to the next. On a related note...

Keep your builds tidy. You might think you have the whole thing in your head now, but if you ever need to go back and change or fix an old build, and you didn't keep everything nice and neat, it's going to be a huge headache to remember what everything does.

Use a different color or type of block for different parts of your build. This will help you keep track of the different sections much more easily.

Use signs to label parts of builds if possible.

The more parts, the bigger the build, the more likely something will go wrong. That's not to say that big builds are bad, but it's worth keeping in mind. Strive for compactness.

Think about the build in different directions when you're stuck or trying to make it better. Would it work better to use vertical gates instead of horizontal, or vice versa?

Updates will mess up Redstone builds. This also just happens. You can always load your build in an older version, but remaking it in the new one is a great way to learn how the new rules work.

General Tips For Wiring Up Your Build

There are many, many ways to build every kind of gate and circuit. There may be a better way to build the one you need for this particular build.

Repeaters can often replace wire, and sometimes should. Their ability to keep the current flowing in only one direction means you can literally place separate lines of power right next to each other, which would never work with Redstone Dust. The extra cost is sometimes well worth it.

Follow the Minecraft Wiki's advice when trying to decide what gate you need for a section of a build: write down all of the inputs that you could have going into the section from the rest of your build, and then take that list and write down all the different possible combinations of power you could create with those. Then look at our section on gates (specifically the parts where it gives the output possibilities, like ON + ON = OFF) and find the gate you want that will use the inputs you have and create the right output.

Pretty much any kind of signal you need can be created, whether it needs to pulse in a particular pattern, be on for a particular amount of time or have a particular strength. Keep looking for the right design for the signal you need.

Test things in Creative Mode before trying them on a real build. Fitting Redstone into almost any real build is hard on its own, but if you're not familiar with what you're trying to make, it's almost always going to cause you problems.

Use Redstone simulation and mapping programs to try out layouts for Redstone without actually having to go into the game and make them. This is great for big builds, or even just getting out of the typical mindset of building in the game, which can give you new perspectives on a build both literally and figuratively. Even just sketching builds on paper is a great idea.

Don't be put off by another builder's complex constructions. At some point all of us were newbs, and most stuff is pretty easily explained if you break it down into parts. That being said, some people are actual engineers, so they have literally studied this stuff. Speaking of...

Learning about engineering and logic rules outside of Minecraft will help your builds get better like nothing else will. If you like Redstone, you should consider looking into these subjects.

Backup your saves. This is something you should probably be doing anyway (and though console folks can't do this easily, you do have the option to restart before an autosave). However, with Redstone you have ever so many more possible problems that can happen. Just try rebuilding a section of a Redstone build after even a small portion of your work has become damaged, much less after a Creeper has decided to go all splodey on it.

Someone out there has tried to build the same thing as you, or something similar. Creating your own way is great, but stealing pieces of other peoples' Redstone builds is part of the tradition. Go look online and see what other people have done to solve the problem. Copying outright is also fine, but never take credit for someone else's invention unless you've changed it significantly to make it your own.

PLACE THE TNT LAST. YOU DO NOT WANT TO EXPLODE.

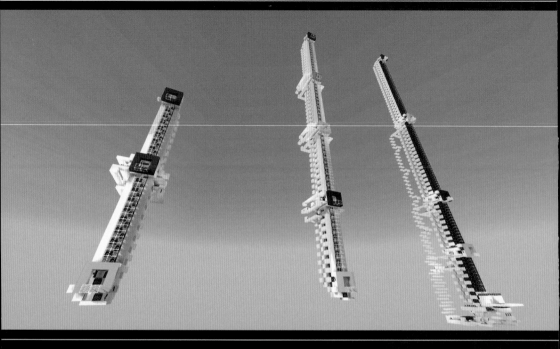

The Redstone **Mechanic Hall of Geniuses**

We think every Redstone engineer is awesome in their own right, but it's gotta be said, some of you builders out there are really insanely good at Redstone. It's outright, unabashedly mind-boggling what some people create with this stuff, and that's why we felt it was our duty to include a chapter honoring some of the best Redstone engineers around and their amazing creations.

Give these guys a look when you're looking for inspiration, and remember: all of these folks once knew nothing about Redstone, just like everyone else. It can be said for certain that they know just a bit more now.

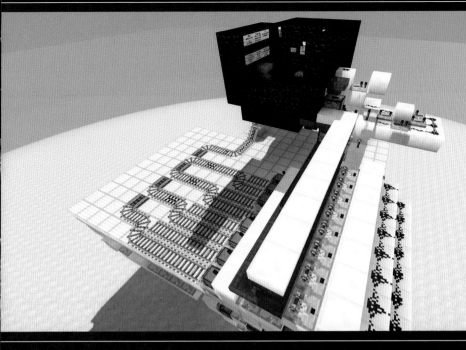

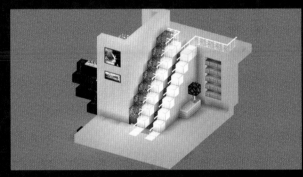

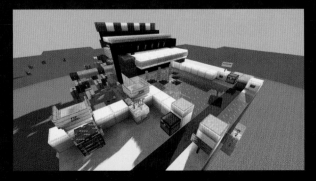

ACtennisAC

youtube.com/user/ACtennisAC/videos

A YouTuber as well as a Minecraft engineer, ACtennisAC makes medium-to-small sized builds that are functional as well as typically meant to be quite fun. For instance, the build you see here in the left hand corner is a working bowling alley game that allows the player to throw "balls" across the Ice and into holes, which sit in front of "pins." When you get the ball in the hole, it registers as knocking down a pin. There are usually a lot of neat little aesthetic touches with ACtennisAC as well, such as the snack machines to the left of the bowling alley.

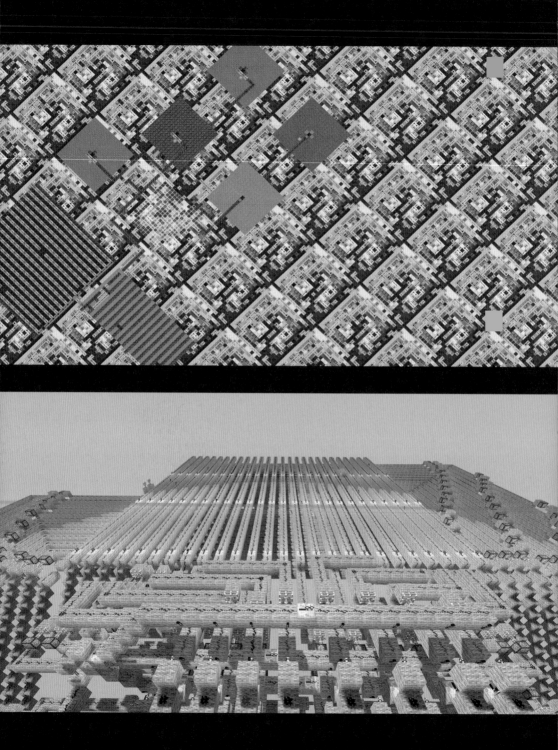

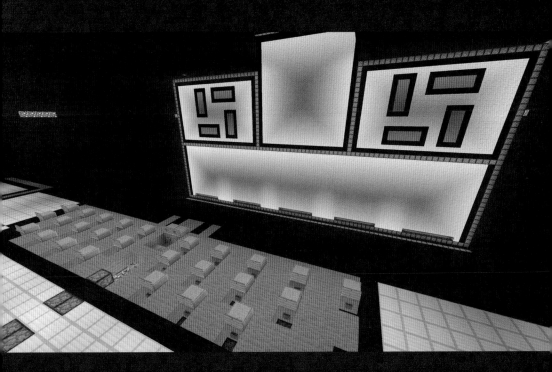

This is a working Hangman mini-game created by Asdjke. Pretty fun, and looks great too!

Asdjke
youtube.com/user/AsdjkeAndBro

His name might look like someone just randomly pounded the keyboard to get it, but there's nothing random at all about Asdjke's builds. Just look at the image at the top of p 174...now that is some absolutely insane Redstoning! What you're looking at there is an enormous creation that actually manufactures random 16x16 chunks of world that look like the normal Minecraft world, including having plants and even ore veins. That's right: Asdjke recreated with Redstone something that usually requires the actual programming of the game to happen. If that's not genius, we don't know what is.

CNB's popular "Gold Rush" mini-game.

CNB

youtube.com/user/CNBMinecraft

CNB is a Crafter out of the UK that is really, really good at making very useful Redstone builds. They also dabble a bit in mini-games and the like, as many Redstone engineers do, but perhaps their best work are their doors, clocks, elevators and builds that actually do something. If you ever are curious as to how to make a functioning "digital" Redstone clock that actually displays numbers, head to CNB's page on PlanetMinecraft and check out their 12hr Digital Clock world, which shows you how to make one that is surprisingly compact.

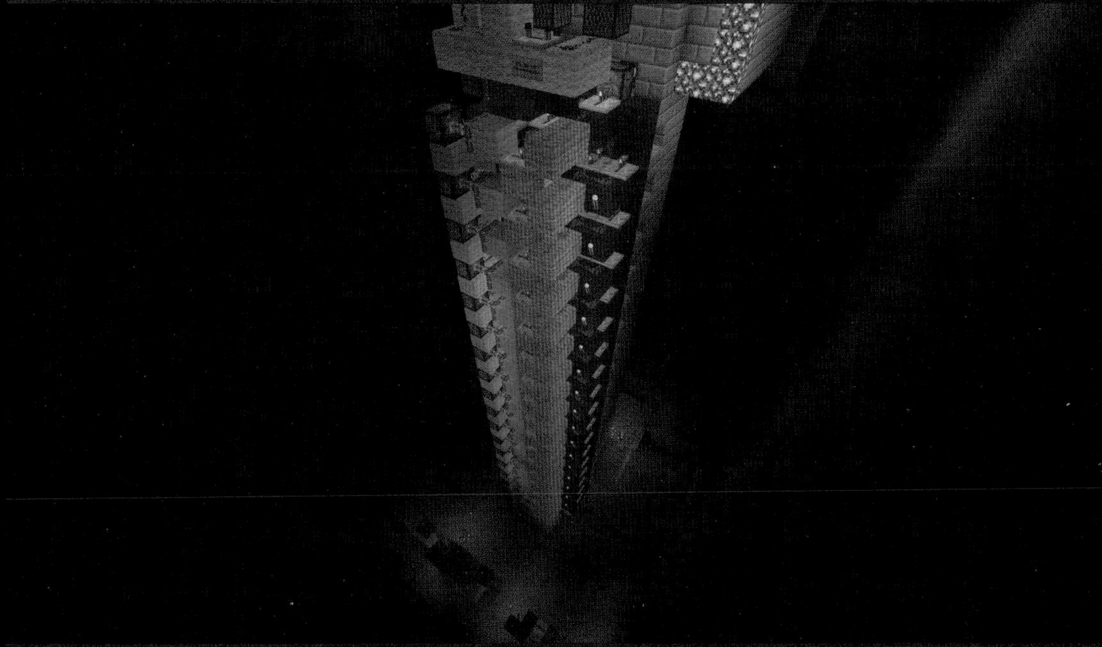

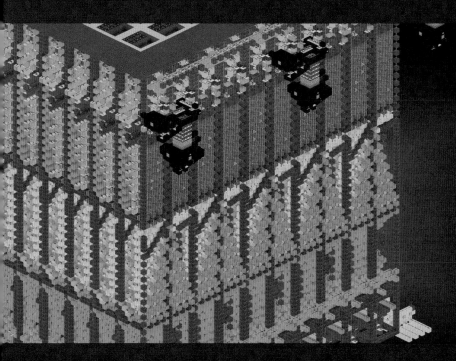

Check out how codecrafted uses different colors of Wool blocks in order to keep track of the various parts of this build, and how spectacular that makes it look in the end. We love this kind of clean work!

codecrafted
codecrafted.net

The user known as codecrafted is one of those builders whose builds not only do something neat, like recreate *Temple Run* in Minecraft or make a hidden door in a Jungle Tree, they also work so efficiently that just looking at their builds is like looking at a piece of Redstone art. codecrafted is incredibly prolific, with 4 whole pages of builds on PlanetMinecraft that range from small, functional doors to some of the biggest Redstone builds we've ever seen. As an example, just look at the build above! What you can see here is just one teeny little bit of one of codecrafted's worlds.

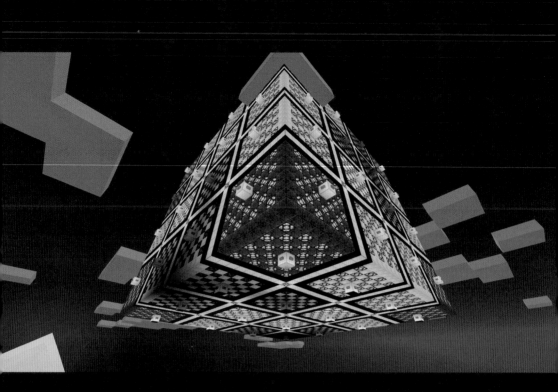

This is Cubehamster's Puzzle Challenge Lights Out build, which think looks quite striking indeed when set against the evening sky.

Cubehamster
youtube.com/user/cubehamster

Cubehamster is pretty darn decent at all things Redstone, but they stand out among the pack in recent days for their work with the new Block of Slime (aka Slimeblock). Using this fun and odd item, Cubehamster has created some of the very best and most creative flying machines around, one of which you see on the bottom of page 181. Something to take away from Cubehamster's work is that working with Redstone does not necessarily mean that one has to sacrifice the look of a build; you can make something functional and awesome-looking too!

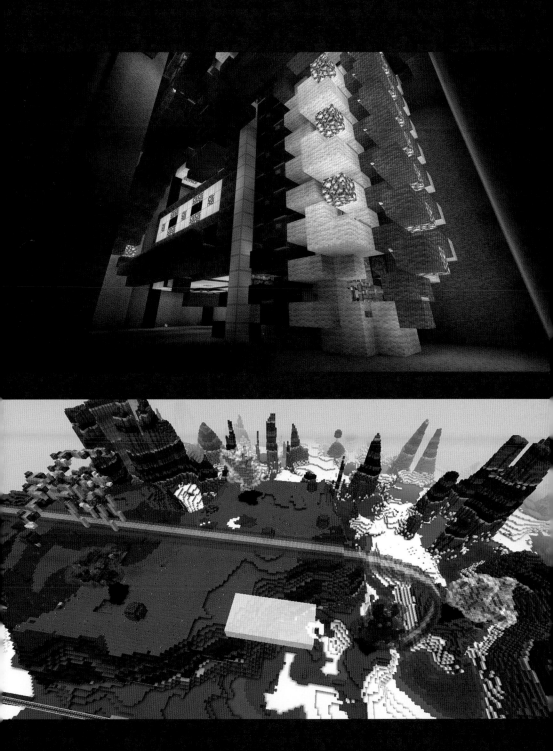

Screenshot: Minecraft® ™ & © 2009–2013 Mojang/Notch.

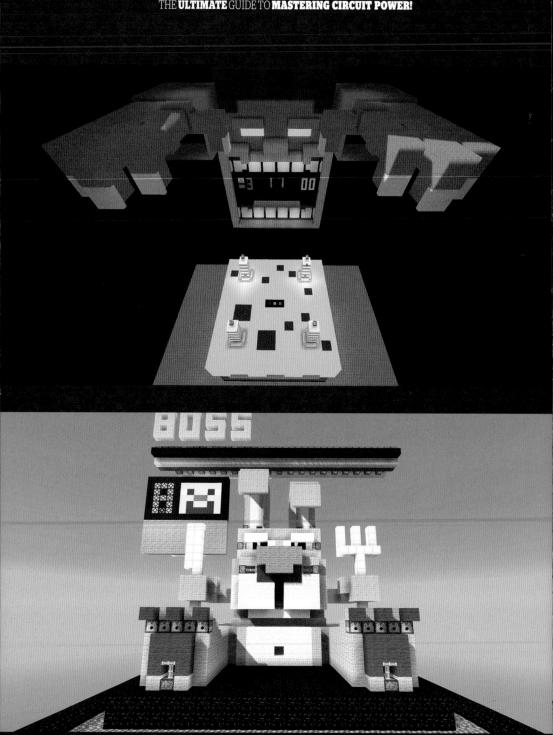

The Redstone Mechanic Hall of Geniuses

That's right: a playable, working guitar in Minecraft, made with Note Blocks. Our hats off to you, Mr. Disco. One really cool thing to note about Disco's builds is that he often leaves Redstone exposed, but builds it in a way that fits the aesthetic of the build and doesn't just look raw and confusing. Which, we don't have to tell you, is quite hard to do.

Disco
ocddisco.com

So, we love every builder in our Hall of Geniuses, but we think even the other guys here would agree that there's something special about the way that Disco's mind works. Disco is a true Redstone pioneer, both for the light-hearted nature of the subject of his builds, and for his serious approach to beautiful, efficient and compact Redstone engineering. The man is not just a great mini-game builder, and not just a bit of a musical genius as well (he has made many playable Redstone instruments), he's even created what is without a doubt one of the most gorgeous Minecraft texture packs ever made. It's called the oCd Texture Pack, and it and many of Disco's truly legendary maps are available at Disco's website. We highly suggest grabbing it, and at least the Cake Defense 2 mini-game while you're at it.

Elevators are hard in Minecraft, but pg5 make it look like a piece of cake all while keeping up their typical aesthetic flair.

pg5
youtube.com/user/minecraftpg5

It probably won't surprise you to hear this confirmed, but it realllllllly helps you be a Redstone genius if you're already an engineer. Or, in the case of pg5, a few engineers. The Minecrafting Redstone group from Germany, pg5, know exactly how all of their builds work, and they have many, many of them that people can check out on PlanetMinecraft (over 100!). The modus operandi with pg5 seems to be that they just have ideas, try them out with Redstone, and get them perfect just about every time. A pg5 build is very easy to recognize for their signature use of many white blocks to hold their builds, such as Quartz and Iron blocks, and they are beautiful not just for their looks, but for their efficiency and elegance with Redstone as well.

The Redstone Mechanic Hall of Geniuses

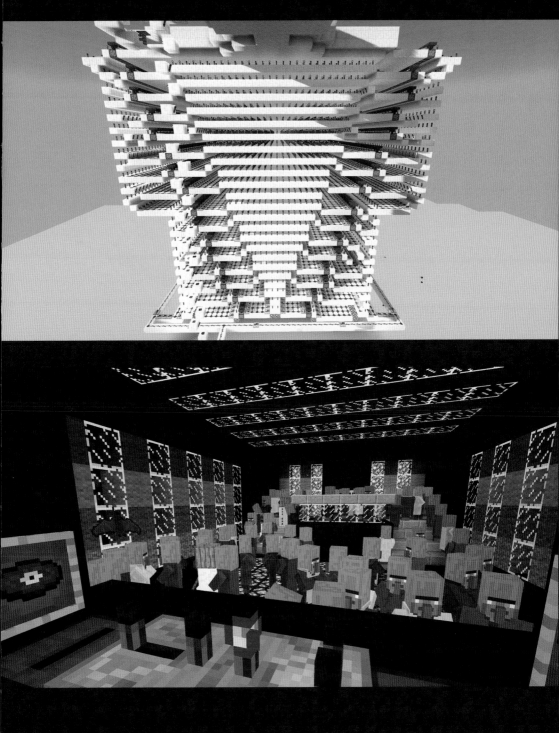

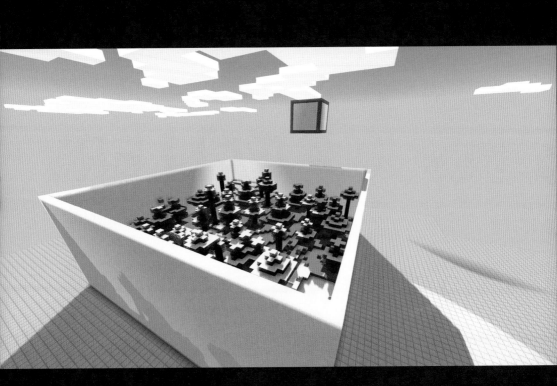

Mini-games are perhaps where Seth's work shines the best, and you can find many to download at his website.

SethBling

sethbling.com

SethBling is not just a Redstone genius, and not even just a former Microsoft engineer, he's also a bonafide Minecraft celebrity. As a member of the famous (and sometimes infamous) MindCrack team, a group of quite talented YouTubers and Minecraft players, SethBling has become one of the most well-known and well-respected figures in the community of Minecraft at large. That is impressive on its own, as is his gameplay, but it's his work with Redstone that makes SethBling a shoo-in as a member of our Hall of Geniuses. Seth has created build after famous, much-downloaded Redstone build, and he's even kind enough to show us all how to recreate much of what he comes up with on his YouTube channel. Thanks SethBling!

Redstone **GALLERY**

Ready for a little more inspiration? We've scoured the web for downloads of the coolest, crispest, cleanest Redstone builds we could find, and we jumped in them and took a few nice shots to show them off to you.

These are examples of some of the infinitely varied things you can do with Redstone, including the traditional (cannons and mini-games), the weird (working iPhone), and the just plain gorgeous (Zephirr's labyrinth!).

All of the builds you see here are available online to download and play in yourself (mostly at the venerable PlanetMinecraft.com), and you should definitely go grab a couple if for no other reason than to see how some of the rules and constructs we've shown you work when done in a successful build.

After looking at all of these sweet, sweet Redstone builds, what are you gonna build next?

300 Block TNT Launcher
by OliverFrenchie

Taking the traditional cannon and turning it a bit on its head is this quite efficient 300 Block
TNT Launcher, which makes you the ammo. Launchers are pretty common, though not so
much as regular cannons, and this one is one of the best we've seen. The 300 blocks refers to
the height you go, and it definitely works; we tried it. A few times.

Something about rows and rows of
Redstone computer parts at night
just looks cool as can be.

Amazing Redstone Computer
by MCPrimeRS

It's all right there in the title: this thing is amazing. It looks cool enough, but this baby is as
fully functional as it is fully freakin' huge. There are a lot of versions of Minecraft computers
out there that folks have made, but not that many of them are as nice as this one, or
available to download and jump about in. If you want to really blow your mind with some
Redstone, download this puppy and fly around a bit. We guarantee you'll be impressed.

This fella's ready to be ridden off into the sunset after you've freed him from his Redstone-y prison.

Automatic Horse Garage
by BrickPig

Sometimes a Redstone build doesn't have to be all that useful or be a purely technical beast. Sometimes it's the most fun just to take a goofy idea and run with it to see if you can make it work. Thus, the Automatic Horse Garage. This thing definitely works too, as it will pop out a Horse for ya in no time. It's also pretty funny to fly around and see the lil horsies penned up, just waitin' to be dispensed.

When downloading Redstone builds, we always suggest flying around the back side to see what makes it tick.

BlockRider
by Brutec

There's no shortage of Redstone mini-games out there waiting to be played, but not many come across with as much style and fun as BlockRider. The idea to use a Minecart as a controllable car is just pure entertainment, and the guts of this thing are very cool to look at as well. Check out that car storage system hanging out underneath!

If you're lucky enough to have some friends to play Minecraft with, and a server to play on, you can't go wrong spending a few hours trying out various mini-games like this. Even better if your friends want to learn Redstone, so you can explore the creation together and to figure out its brains!

Connect Four
by FillzMinecraft

Another solid mini-game build, this is a recreation of the beloved kid's game Connect Four that uses Redstone Lamps to indicate which slots have been used. Using Lamps as indicators like this, or even as whole screens, is fairly common, but also pretty freakin' complex. Just look at how much Redstone this bad boy has pouring out the back of it.

FaSOlka is a beast, but is has to be for it to have this many options.

FaSOlka III
by remixis098

We definitely had to throw another Redstone computer in here, and this time it's a bit different from our last. FaSOlka III is actually a computer-like build that is made to be a simulation of a music studio, and it does produce real music when you use it! There are a great many controls inside of FaSOlka III, allowing everything from multiple sequences to even selecting different instruments.

This build looks like it doesn't take much Redstone, but that's because the mighty Command Block is used for some of the functions.

Herobrine Boss Battle by SpeedyCrafting

Those of you who have been Crafting for a while are probably quite familiar with Herobrine, but for those who aren't, he's Minecraft's resident legendary boogieman. It's pretty traditional to build Redstone mini-games that focus around the legend of Herobrine, and this one here by SpeedyCrafting is one of our favorites. It's a giant room that pits you against traps and mobs and parkour and more, and getting out alive is no easy feat.

Hidden Tree Door
by codecrafted

We already talked about the great codecrafted and their myriad builds in our Hall of Geniuses, but we like them so much, we felt our Gallery needed a touch of the old CC as well. One of the many builds available on PlanetMinecraft, this Hidden Tree Door showcases everything that codecrafted is good at- it's a functional, compact and creative little build.

What do we have here? It wouldn't be our friend the NOT gate, would it? Of course it would; NOT gates are everywhere in Redstone builds!

Little do you know when you see Le Labyrinthe from its humble facade just how big and complex the monster maze you're about to enter really is.

Le labyrinthe de Zephirr

Oh my. So this thing is impressive, even compared to some of our Hall of Geniuses builds. Zephirr has done something truly awesome here, which is to create a giant maze that constantly changes which hallways are open inside of it while you're in it. It's huge, it's incredibly hard to solve, and it works like a charm. Plus, looking at it from above (you're seeing the roof of it right here) is one of the most mesmerizing things we've ever done in this game.

Everything works on this rig!

LPG's Redstone Computer

Another big boy of a computer, LPG has really shown off some creative flair with this build by creating it to not only work like a computer, but to actually look like one too! As LPG himself says, "Redstone to the max. This computer contains a 6x4 letter display that can display 1-9, A-Z as well as other things." We think the details on the tower are a nice touch. Definitely check this one out at PlanetMinecraft.com

When you win, Fireworks shoot off in the same colors as the code you solved! What a great touch.

Mastermind
by SimNico

Mastermind is a throwback to an old board game about breaking codes with the same name, and SimNico has faithfully given the old game a nice update using Redstone. In SimNico's version, Wool blocks of different colors replace the pegs from the original, and players can challenge each other without having to track down a physical copy of the board, which is pretty darn neat.

Mega Gargantua
by Codehamster

Like with codecrafted's tree, we just couldn't pass up an opportunity to talk more about CubeHamster, specifically their Mega Gargantua. So look at this thing for a minute. Just take in how big it is and how many pieces it has. Now let us tell you: this thing walks. Yes, it actually moves. The whole thing. And, it fires cannons out of its front. It is the coolest. Of all time.

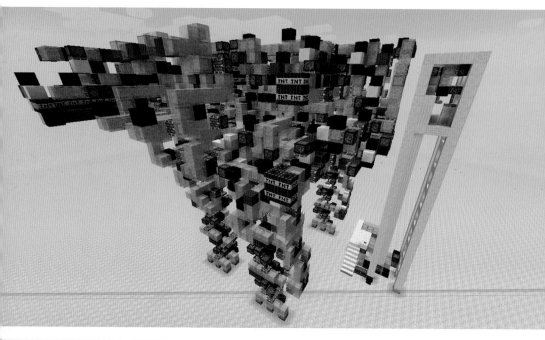

Many have tried their hand at moving creations now that the Slimeblock is around, but few have ever succeeded on such a scale as the Mega Gargantua does.

Looks like that pesky Herobrine has been racking up some time with noah-daniels' game. Better get practicin' on this guy, can't let Herobrine win!

Minigame
by noah-daniels

It might not have a flashy name, but Minigame is a perfect example of how to make Redstone work to create something fun and simple. This game takes skill and is quick to play but hard to master, and it actually keeps score for you on the screen using Command Block features.

Peter's Working iPhone

This thing is not lying in the title: it does work, it does act like an iPhone, and we suppose Peter did build it (though we don't know Peter, so who knows). This build is pretty amazing from a technical standpoint: it uses Wool blocks that are moved around quickly to make the things happen on the screen. Even crazier, you control it with actual touch controls by running around on it. It even has a tutorial that shows you everything you can do, which includes opening and using all sorts of apps!

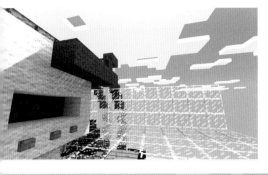

Reaction Time Minigame
by Flancake

We wrap our Gallery of builds with another little, yet impressive one. Flancake, who has probably the best Minecraft name ever, has done a lot with just a little Redstone here, and that makes this build an ideal one to get in as a beginner to see how some of the subjects we've talked about are used in real builds. For instance, check out that Glowstone ladder on the right. We told you those would come in handy!

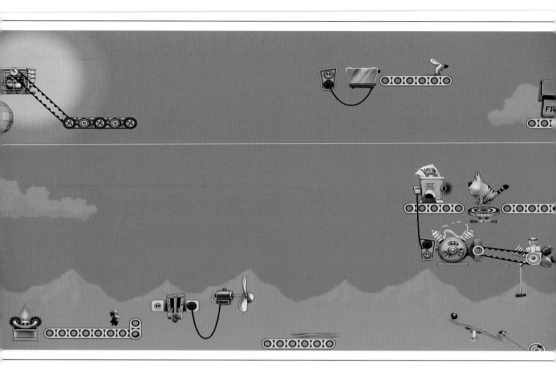

Wiring Up In Other
Building Games

Redstone is, in our heavily biased opinion, the greatest wiring and logic simulator in any video game ever made, but it's far from being the only one out there. In recent years, and partially inspired by Redstone's success, many other games have added the ability to use user-created systems to achieve effects and goals, both logical and mechanical. These games range from those that are all about the contraptions (such as, unsurprisingly, Contraption Maker), to those that just have a little wiring included in them for some added kicks and complexity (like Terraria).

If the ole Redstone wiring bug has gotcha, and you're looking to create more machines and simulations with a whole new set of rules and tools, these are the games you'll want to check out.

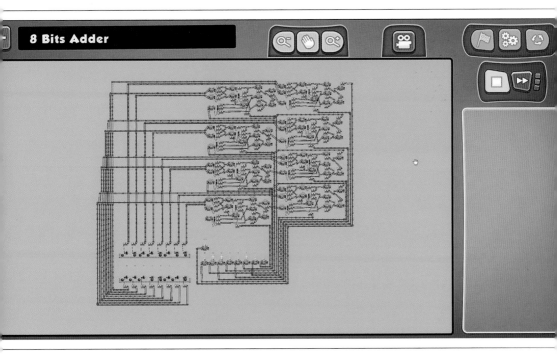

Contraption Maker

Contraption Maker is probably the most different game here from Minecraft, and also from the rest of the games on this list. Instead of creating machines by using rules that are based mostly in logic or recreating electronics and/or real-life physical machinery, *Contraption Maker's* whole goal is for players to build Rube Goldberg-esque machines that perform functions in very goofy and unexpected ways.

The basic game of *CM* involves manipulating already built machines, adding and subtracting from them to solve physical puzzles, but its creation mechanism allows players to manipulate a pretty huge spread of items and systems, from physical ones like pulleys and levers to electrical and more. It's made by some of the same people that brought us the classic *The Incredible Machine* game, and being a game that is exclusively about various items and how they interact with each other to get results, people have built everything you can think of and more in CM, including adders.

CM is a great game for those that would like to focus just on the machine and contraption building, and ditch the first-person and other game components from the rest of these games. It works great in this way, because that's the whole point of the game, as opposed to being a subsystem. Definitely worth the money of any virtual engineer.

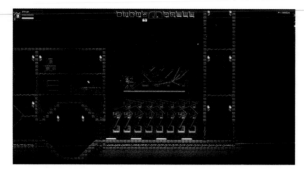

Terraria
If you're a building-game aficionado, then Terraria is already well-known to you. This indie, side-scrolling builder/explorer game is well-loved for its sense of adventure and massive amount of items, but people often overlook its fairly complex wiring system.

Terraria's wiring doesn't feature as many items as Minecraft's, and builds can't get quite as intensive, but it does feature some *Terraria*-specific items that fit very well into its aesthetic of playful adventure. For instance, statues in Terraria can be hooked up to wiring systems to activate special functions like spawning power-ups or mobs. And don't get us wrong; a lot can be done with *Terraria's* wiring system, and the game itself is well worth a look for any Minecraft fan.

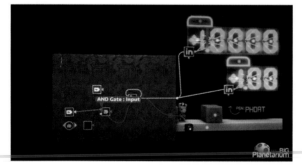

Little Big Planet
You might be surprised to see this ultra-fun and lighthearted family game on our list, but don't be fooled by *LBP's* cutesy look! There's a very powerful creation engine in this game, and the ability to use it to create one's own levels allows for some very interesting things to be made.

LBP players can actually create Redstone-esque builds like adding machines and more in two ways: with its quite well-made and reliable physics engine, or with built-in wiring concepts such as pre-made logic gates. In the physics versions, players essentially recreate physical input/output machines by building a structure that utilizes physical versions of things like logic gates that function by using the rules of gravity to act on items and get resulting outputs. People have built many neat constructs with just this feature alone, including, as mentioned, adding machines. The actual wiring side of LBP, on the other hand, is similar to Starbound's, in that you can wire up power sources to pre-made logic gates and then mechanisms to achieve various cool results.

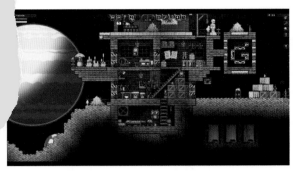

Starbound

As you might notice from the similarities in their looks, side-scroller space exploration game *Starbound* is by the same folks who make Terraria, a company named Chucklefish, and it too has a wiring system in its mechanics. However, *Starbound* fulfills the expectations of a more tech-based game by really ramping up its wiring system quite heavily compared to Terraria's.

There are a pretty huge amount of wiring items in *Starbound*, including dozens of "switches" (think power components), items that respond to the power (think mechanisms) and even some pre-built logic gates. It's still not the level of customizability that Redstone has, but it's a very powerful wiring system.

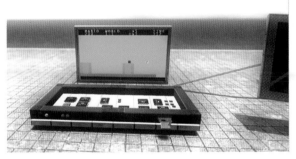

Wiremod for Garry's Mod

When it comes to competing with Redstone for complexity and the ability to build simulations of real electronics systems, the Wiremod for the Source-engine based sandbox/physics game called *Garry's Mod* is heads and tails above the rest. *Garry's Mod* isn't really a game with a specific goal; instead it just gives players a sandbox world with various rules and items, which they use to create anything in their heads. It's somewhat similar to Minecraft in that way, but imagine instead of Minecraft's voxel-based boxy look and playfulness, Garry's Mod is based on more reality-style first-person shooter models and physics.

Wiremod is a modification program for *Garry's Mod* that is, according to its Steam page, "A collection of entities connectable by data wires, which allows for the creation of advanced contraptions." And when they say advanced, they are not exaggerating at all- Wiremod has been used to create everything from semi-functioning but highly realistic models of real-life classic cars to virtual models of computers that actually look quite like a regular computer. If you like the technical aspects of Redstone and want to focus more on that and less on the block-placing, Wiremod is definitely the next step.

THE **ULTIMATE** GUIDE TO
MASTERING
CIRCUIT
POWER!

MINECRAFT®™ REDSTONE and the Keys to Supercharging Your Builds in Sandbox Games

This book is available in quantity at special discounts for your group or organization.
For further information, contact:

Triumph Books LLC
814 North Franklin Street
Chicago, Illinois 60610
Phone: (312) 337-0747
www.triumphbooks.com

Printed in U.S.A.
ISBN: 978-1-62937-094-1

Content packaged by Mojo Media, Inc.
Joe Funk: Editor
Jason Hinman: Creative Director
Trevor Talley: Writer